PROMOTES FUTUR...

HOLLYWOOD FILMS

PUBLICIZES

PROVIDES THEATRICAL RELE...

BUILDS QUALITY

PROVIDES IMAGE

CREATES

CREATES NEW DISNEY FANS

CREATES AND PRODUCES

PROVIDES ADDITIONAL OUTLET FOR

PROVIDES ART FOR

PROMOTES FILMS AND STARS

PROVIDES ART FOR

FEEDS FILM TO

ART FOR... STARS

FEEDS TUNES A...

KEEPS

WALT DISNEY STUDIO

CONTENTS

INTRODUCTION

Creativity is never in short supply at the Walt Disney Studios. Walt was the undisputed master storyteller, and he surrounded himself with men and women whose creative genius complemented and sometimes rivaled his own—a legacy that continues to this day.

At Disney, we often say that our imaginations know no boundaries. But historically, that's not quite true. Over time, the more-or-less "happy problem" wasn't about finding and executing ideas, but about just finding a place big enough to realize them. Throughout the history of The Walt Disney Company, which is now nearing the centennial mark, its artists and storytellers have faced a chronic dilemma: constantly needing more space to stretch the limits of the mind and meet the need for growth.

It all began in the summer of 1923, when Walt Disney boarded the Santa Fe's *California Limited* in Kansas City, Missouri's Union Station. At that moment, his studio was comprised of his singular creative vision and the contents of the pasteboard suitcase he carried with him. But a short time after his arrival in Hollywood, Disney's dreams took root in his Uncle Robert's garage, and he soon sold the concept of his Alice Comedies cartoon series to a distributor. With the help of his brother Roy O. Disney, who would remain his lifelong business partner, the Disney Studios was off to the races.

Taking up shop in the rear of a small storefront in the Los Feliz area of Los Angeles, Walt ramped up production on the Alice series, and within four months his staff grew; so, he then moved into the empty storefront next

Walt Disney draws a Mickey Mouse advertisement at the Hyperion studio (c. 1930).

Walt Disney walks past the Animation Building in Burbank (1940s).

THE *Walt Disney* STUDIOS

A Lot to Remember

View of the Walt Disney Studios, Burbank, from the Griffith Park hills,
April 11, 1940.

For information address Disney Editions,
1200 Grand Central Avenue, Glendale, California 91201.

Editorial Director: Wendy Lefkon
Executive Editor: Laura Hopper
Designed by Margie Peng

ISBN 978-1-368-05178-1
FAC-029191-19158
Library of Congress Control Number: 2015043643
Printed in Malaysia
Second Edition, January 2019
1 3 5 7 9 10 8 6 4 2

Visit www.disneybooks.com

The Official Disney Fan Club
D23.com

THE WALT DISNEY STUDIOS

A Lot to Remember

STEVEN CLARK • REBECCA CLINE

EDITIONS

LOS ANGELES • NEW YORK

This book is dedicated to
Maggie, Andy, and Jackson—

the joy Disney brings to your eyes warms our hearts.
That's the magic of Disney.

Early animation staff at the Hyperion studio—from front left: Jack King, Norm Ferguson, and Dick Lundy. From front right: Ben Sharpsteen, Merle Gilson, and Bert Gillett (c. 1929).

door. This, however, would turn out to be a temporary solution.

By 1925, Walt and Roy had put a down payment on a weed-infested lot in the same Los Feliz district (which is nestled between Hollywood and Glendale) that their studio was based in. There they built the Hyperion studio—the place where Mickey, Donald, Goofy, and the gang were born, as was the fairest of them all, Snow White. But once again, quarters quickly became cramped, inefficient, cluttered, and uncomfortable. Despite numerous expansions, Hyperion remained a patchwork quilt of sorts and was ultimately unsuited for effective animation production operations. It was again time to move and start nearly from scratch—at least location-wise.

In 1938, Walt did just that. He put down a deposit on fifty-one acres to the north of Hyperion Avenue, where the studios were located, but outside Los Angeles in the town of Burbank, California. The land was a clean slate, and the

perfect site for his new, idyllic production facility. It would be a completely modern plant designed specifically for the purpose and special needs associated with animation production. By the time construction was complete and the entire staff had moved onto the new lot, it was the fall of 1940.

According to Bill Garity, a pioneering film engineer whom Walt assigned to spearhead the planning and construction of the Burbank project, once the move was completed and there was a period of adjustment, "The Disney Studios find their new home admirably suited for the varied and complex demands of fine motion-picture production. Time has proven its flexibility and its capacity for expansion. The physical plant has proven an excellent instrument . . . for Walt Disney, his artists and technicians, and will, no doubt, be the source of many inspiring spectacles to come."

Walt Disney Productions, as it was then called, was spacious and spectacular, bustling but surprisingly serene. These were busy, often frenetic times, and by the 1950s the studio enjoyed good fortune on all fronts. The company was capable of handling it, thanks to the lot's initial master plan, which had been imagined and constructed with expansion in mind. Walt and his staff had a wellspring of ideas just waiting to be realized, and within this halcyon era, it's safe to say that the Burbank studio was earning its reputation as the world's epicenter for imagination.

Ultimately, though, Disney would again find itself bursting at the seams creatively and physically—even with a master plan for such an occurrence in place. But how could it not? Walt Disney's once small animation studio had diversified. All at once, Walt was actively producing animated features, animated short subjects, live-action films, television series and specials, and, of course, developing and constructing an all-new concept in themed family amusements called Disneyland.

Yet as the years have unfolded, Garity's prediction and faith in the lot's capabilities continue to ring true for the most part: on the Burbank lot, spectacles have indeed been in abundant supply. From *Cinderella* to *Frozen*, *Davy Crockett* to *Home Improvement*, *Mary Poppins* to *Pirates of the Caribbean*, and the *Mark Twain Riverboat* to the *Matterhorn*, decade after decade and amazement upon amazement, Disney has yet to show its age, remaining a

youthful, exuberant storyteller and generous source of creativity and inspiration for the young and young at heart, wherever they may be. And the company's Burbank facility's capacity remains the hub for nearly all this activity.

The once sleepy hamlet of Burbank was indeed (and remains) home to a plant that manufactured the rarest of commodities: magic. It was something the world had—and has (when something new is unveiled)—never seen before. Seventy-five years after opening its gates, the Walt Disney Studios, which is today the headquarters for the entire Disney organization, continues to be the heart of Disney's rich legacy and exciting future.

As Walt once said, "Disneyland will never be completed as long as there is imagination left in the world." One could argue that this famous promise applies to far more than just Disneyland; it's to all the creative endeavors that bear the Disney name.

In the pages that follow, we celebrate Walt Disney's dream factory and its seven-and-a-half-decade reign over the imaginations, hearts, and minds of millions of people around the world who have been inspired by the optimism, decency, and magic of Disney.

Steven Clark and Rebecca Cline

Front gate of the Walt Disney Studios,
500 S. Buena Vista St., Burbank, CA.

Aerial shot of the Walt Disney Studios in Burbank (1946).

THE FLEDGLING STUDIOS

Hyperion studio courtyard (1937).

I n the years before building the sprawling
Southern California campus in Burbank,
with its perfectly manicured lawns,
whimsically designed buildings, and ultramodern
soundstages, Walt Disney made do in an array
of outlets, including his parents' Kansas City
garage. The year was 1921 and Walt, at just
twenty years old, was beginning a journey that
would eventually lead him to the very top of the
entertainment world.

His boss at the Kansas City Film Ad Company
at the time loaned him a used camera, an
exceedingly generous gesture given the cost
of such equipment in those days. Walt had
promptly built a camera stand and begun
tinkering. (As a child, he'd dreamt of becoming an
actor until stumbling upon a "how-to" book on
the budding field of animation at his local library.
From that point on, he was hooked.)

Before long, Walt and colleague Fred Harman
started their own fledgling cartoon company,
Kaycee Studios, in a tiny rented shop at
Thirtieth and Holmes streets. There, amid
the shaking and clatter from the streetcar
barn directly below, Walt and Fred tested
new techniques for making animated theater
commercials. By the spring of 1922, Walt had
completed the first in a series of silent animated
shorts that came to be called Laugh-O-grams.

The first cartoons, *Little Red Riding Hood*
and *The Four Musicians of Bremen*, were fairy
tales with a modern twist, a formula that would
serve Walt well in the years to follow. They
were successful enough to allow him to quit his
day job and focus solely on creating his first
legitimate animation studio. The incorporation
of that studio, which Walt rechristened Laugh-O-
gram Films, included five financial investors and
a move to larger digs at the McConahy Building
at 1127 East Thirty-first Street in Kansas City.
Walt rented a second-floor suite and hired ten
artists to produce and market the new series.

The Laugh-O-gram studio was an exuberant
enterprise from the start. Walt's young staff—
some still in their teens—shared his passion for
animation. But such enthusiasm wasn't enough
to keep the studio profitable. Compounding
matters, his distributor, Pictorial Clubs, Inc., went
bust while still owing Walt more than $11,000 for
completed shorts. He desperately reached out to

Disney staff members pose in front of the Disney Bros.
Studio on Kingswell Avenue in 1925. Left to right:
Ub Iwerks, Rollin "Ham" Hamilton, and Walt Disney.

family and friends for loans, a short-term fix that
allowed him to continue work on an innovative
new series.

Inspired by Max Fleisher's popular animated/
live-action hybrid *Out of the Inkwell* series, Walt's
latest venture featured an adorable four-year-
old girl named Alice (played by actress Virginia
Davis), who seeks adventure in a cartoon
"wonderland." As Laugh-O-gram slid inexorably
into bankruptcy, Walt and his remaining staff
raced to finish the pilot, *Alice's Wonderland*.

Discouraged but not downtrodden, Walt
found himself at a crossroads in the summer of
1923. He considered moving to New York before
ultimately deciding, like so many before him, to
test his fortunes in Hollywood. If he couldn't
find success in animation, Walt reasoned,
perhaps he'd have luck as a director or writer in
live-action pictures.

• • •

Walt Disney arrived in Hollywood in August of
1923 with a cheap pasteboard suitcase, his *Alice's
Wonderland* reel, and little else. Undaunted,
the young artist immediately created business
cards and letterhead advertising himself as a
cartoonist using his Uncle Robert's address:
4406 Kingswell Avenue, Los Angeles, CA. He
pounded the pavement in search of studio
jobs and shopped the Alice pilot to various
distributors in Hollywood and New York. While
two months passed without so much as a lead or
response, Walt busied himself in Uncle Robert's

Lillian, Walt, Ruth, Roy, and Edna Disney pose in front of the Disney Bros. Studio on Kingswell Avenue in Los Angeles (1925).

garage, constructing a stand for an animation camera that he'd recently purchased. Finally, in October of 1923, good news arrived via telegram from Miss M. J. Winkler in New York. Winkler, the distributor of both *Felix the Cat* and *Out of the Inkwell*, wanted to buy his series!

Walt raced to the Sawtelle Veterans Hospital in West Los Angeles where his brother Roy, a World War I vet, was recovering from illness. Brimming with enthusiasm, he persuaded Roy to leave the hospital and join him in a brand-new studio venture, Disney Bros. Studio. For the tidy sum of $10 a month, they found office space just down the street from Uncle Robert's house, in the rear of a small office occupied by Holly-Vermont Realty at 4651 Kingswell Avenue; and on October 16, the Disney brothers signed their first contract with Winkler. The company that

would soon become a worldwide household name had officially put down roots.

The contract with Winkler called for one new Alice Comedy a month for the first year, no small feat for two men with limited resources and office space. By January 1924, the Disney Bros. Studio had added five staff members, rented a vacant lot three blocks away at 4589 Hollywood Boulevard and Rodney Drive for outdoor shooting on the Alice films, and expanded to an adjacent storefront at 4649 Kingswell Avenue. But even this additional space proved to be insufficient when, in the contract's second year, Winkler upped their production demand to one Alice short every three weeks. As would so often be the case over the next several decades, the Disney company needed to grow quickly.

Walt and Roy scouted the surrounding neighborhoods, and on July 6, 1925, they finally placed a $400 deposit on a small parcel of land at 2719 Hyperion Avenue in the Los Feliz area of Los Angeles. Construction of the new one-story studio began shortly afterwards in July of 1925 and was completed the following February. Walt and Roy claimed the two partitioned offices, but the bulk of the space was left open for the animation, background, and inking and painting departments.

Over the next three years, the Disney brothers

Scale drawing of the interior of the Disney Bros. Studio on Kingswell Avenue (1970s).

Original graphics for the Disney Bros. Studio on Kingswell Avenue (1920s).

and their team of artists produced fifty-six *Alice Comedies* at the Hyperion studio before signing another contract with Winkler in 1927 for a cartoon series with a brand-new star: Oswald the Lucky Rabbit. He was charming, mischievous, and soon to be immensely popular. Walt and company produced twenty-six Oswald cartoons in the first year, and Walt hoped to secure additional funding from their distributor to improve the animation quality as he headed east to adjust the contract Disney had with Winkler and her new husband and partner, Charles Mintz.

But upon arriving in New York, he discovered that Winkler and Mintz had their own plans for Oswald—ones that didn't include Walt and Roy. The distributor, who owned the rights to the character, planned to drastically reduce the Disney brothers' management role and make the Oswald cartoons in their own studios at what they argued would be a substantially lower cost. And that wasn't the worst of it: Mintz had already hired most of Walt's staff out from under him.

Never one to dwell on setbacks, Walt spent the long train ride heading back west after losing Oswald brainstorming and thinking of a new character. He met with Roy and a few remaining loyal staff members upon his return to map out a plan for the future. With the help

Ink and Paint "girls" take a lunch break on the stairs of the Hyperion studio (1930s).

of his chief animator and friend, Ub Iwerks, Walt went to work creating what would soon become the world's most famous mouse. Unfortunately, the new character also boasted just about the world's worst name—Mortimer—before Walt's wife, Lillian, persuaded him to change it to Mickey. The new name stuck, thankfully, though Walt would go on to use the name Mortimer as one of Mickey Mouse's rivals.

Iwerks animated two silent Mickey Mouse cartoons, *Plane Crazy* and *The Gallopin' Gaucho*, but Walt was unable to find a distributor.

Hyperion artists work on the *Silly Symphonies*; counterclockwise: Johnny Cannon, Jack Cutting, Wilfred Jackson, Ub Iwerks, Les Clark (1929).

PERSONNEL

ANIMATION
1. Merle Gilson
2. Ben Sharpsteen
3. Burt Gillett
4. Jack Cutting
5. Norm Ferguson
6. Dick Lundy
7. Les Clark
8. Ub Iwerks
9. Wilfred Jackson
10. Johnny Cannon
11. Floyd Gottfredson
12. Dave Hand
13. Tom Palmer
14. Jack King

BACKGROUND ARTISTS
15. Carlos Manriquez
16. Emil Flohri

OTHERS
17. Win Smith
18. Bill Cottrell
19. Chuck Couch
20. Hazel Sewell (Cottrell)
21. Carl Stalling
22. Lucille Benedict, Secretary

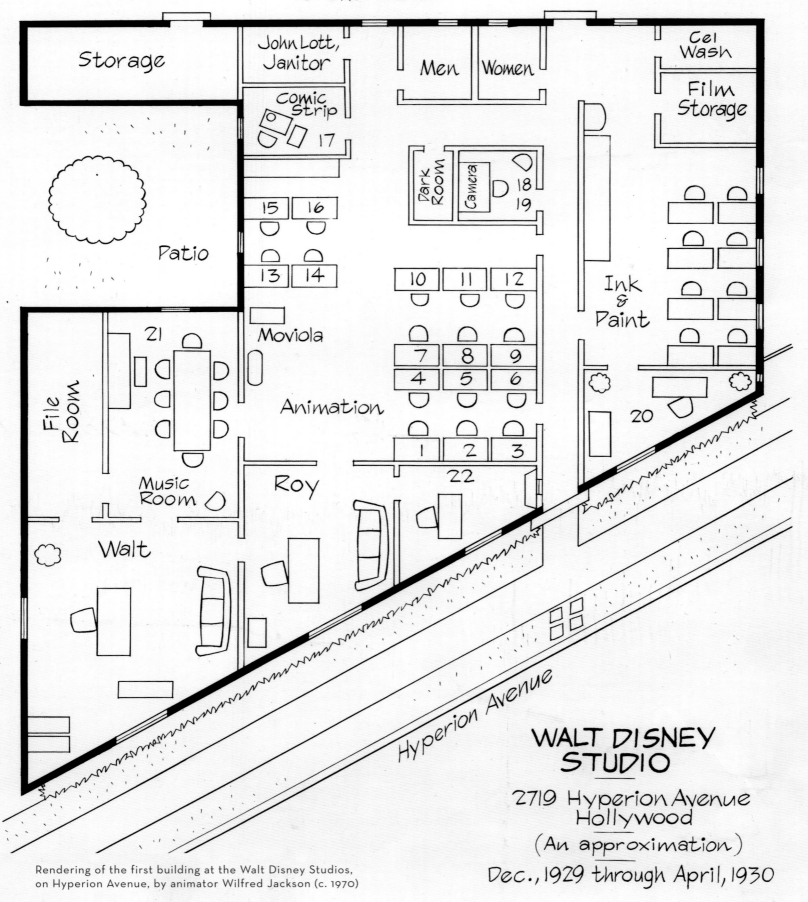

Rendering of the first building at the Walt Disney Studios, on Hyperion Avenue, by animator Wilfred Jackson (c. 1970)

WALT DISNEY STUDIO

2719 Hyperion Avenue
Hollywood
(An approximation)
Dec., 1929 through April, 1930

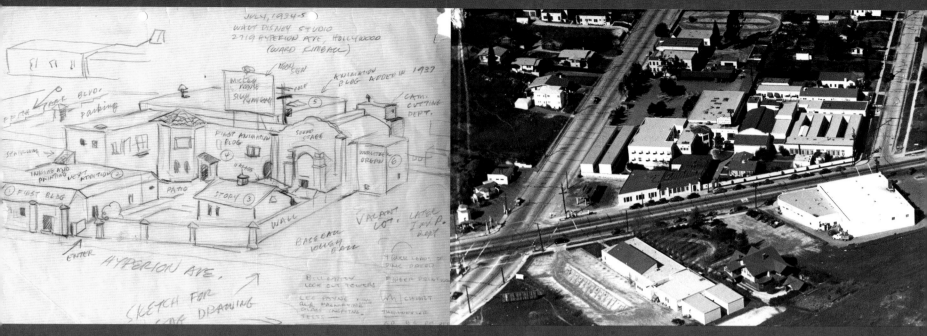

Sketch of the first building at the Walt Disney Studios, on Hyperion Avenue, by animator Ward Kimball (c.1970).

Aerial of the Hyperion studio (c. 1937).

Though only a few years removed from the success of the *Alice Comedies* and Oswald shorts, much had changed in the entertainment world. *The Jazz Singer*, the first motion picture with sound, had premiered in 1927, entrancing theater audiences everywhere. And so it was to be a third cartoon, *Steamboat Willie*, the first animated film to feature fully synchronized sound, that would end up serving as Mickey Mouse's "official" debut. *Steamboat Willie* opened on November 18, 1928, at the Colony Theater in New York. The plucky and playful star of the movie was suddenly an overnight sensation.

Mickey was such a hit, in fact, that his animated adventures couldn't be shipped to theaters fast enough. Walt and his new team of

young, ambitious animators worked nonstop to produce new Mickey shorts while also developing a companion series—the *Silly Symphonies*. These cartoons featured a new cast of characters every time, allowing Walt and his animators to experiment with mood, emotion, and musical themes. When Silly Symphonies also became a hit with audiences, Walt realized it was once again time for the company to expand.

In 1929 and 1930, several additions were made to the Hyperion building, and the following year, a two-story animator's building and soundstage were built on the lot. Walt's new, larger office was housed in the new building, as well as the Disney Film Recording Company, an offshoot of the studio that had been renting space at the

Behind the scenes of *Bambi*—animators Ollie Johnston, Milt Kahl, and Frank Thomas with the voice of Thumper, Peter Behn (1940).

During the filming of *Peculiar Penguins*, a young Walt Disney dangles a fish while cameraman Bill Garity shoots (1930s).

Tec-Art Studios across from the Paramount lot on Melrose Avenue. By the renovation project's end, the Walt Disney Studios ballooned in size from 1,600 square feet of floor space to twenty thousand square feet.

With the expansion complete, Walt turned his attention to a new, even more ambitious endeavor. One night in 1934, he informed his animators of his plan to make an animated feature film—another first in the motion-picture industry. His idea was met with skepticism from the team, but his enthusiasm quickly became infectious.

The project spanned three long years and was so expensive that Hollywood insiders began referring to it as "Disney's Folly." But when *Snow White and the Seven Dwarfs* premiered right before Christmas in 1937, Walt's vision and investment were richly rewarded. The movie earned $8 million dollars at the box office, no small feat when the average theater ticket cost twenty-three cents, and would go on to become the highest-grossing film to date. Critics were equally enchanted, awarding Walt an honorary Oscar for the groundbreaking film.

The success of *Snow White* convinced Walt that there was a market for full-length animated movies, and, as a result, he set a goal of releasing one new animated feature a year moving forward. With several new features in the works and an ongoing slate of lucrative Mickey and Silly Symphony shorts, the Disney lot was bursting at the seams.

Walt and staff in a *Grasshopper and the Ants* story session, Hyperion studio (1934).

Front view of the Walt Disney Studios on Hyperion Avenue (1931).

The Disney Studio staff spill out onto the lawn to rest during their lunch hour (1930s).

The front entrance of the Animation Building at Hyperion studio (1930s).

Hyperion employees take a break under the shade of a tree in the studio parking lot (1939).

The staff of the Walt Disney Studios celebrate the success of Mickey Mouse in the summer of 1932.

JOURNEY TO BURBANK

Walt Disney, in his Hyperion office, pores over Kem Weber's renderings of the new Burbank studio (1939).

In the fall of 1938, word began to spread of a massive construction project being planned for a sprawling tract of land near (but on the other side of) Los Angeles' Griffith Park. Walt Disney, the creator of Mickey Mouse and the astonishingly successful *Snow White and the Seven Dwarfs*, was coming to Burbank!

Glamorous as it may have sounded, the grounds themselves were far less impressive at first glance. "Interested Hollywoodians who trek out to [the] San Fernando Valley to inspect the fifty-one-acre site of Walt Disney's new studio are greeted by one lone squat building and a herd of cows," said Bill Garity, the studio's first production manager, while the Burbank effort was proceeding.

Walt placed a deposit on the Burbank lot on August 31, 1938, but plans for the new "plant," as staffers called it, had been in the works since production on *Snow White* had commenced. Disney's plan to produce one feature a year "meant that three features were to be in work at the same time: one in preliminary stages of story and study; another in the actual process of animation; and a third going through the finishing stages," said Garity.

Eventually, this schedule was amended to a still-ambitious plan of one feature every two years, though this was while still churning out high-quality Mickey and *Silly Symphony* shorts on a regular basis. The old Hyperion lot, which had grown "like Topsy" according to many staffers, simply couldn't handle that level of

A billboard touting the location of the soon-to-be-built Walt Disney Studios at the corner of Alameda Avenue and Buena Vista Street in Burbank (1939).

production, even with the additions that had been made over the last fourteen years.

That expansion had taken place in chaotic fits and starts, quick "Band-Aid" fixes to obstacles the team encountered while in the controlled chaos of production. As such, the Hyperion lot suffered from something akin to suburban sprawl. Animators' desks looked more like animators' stalls; the screening room was referred to, appropriately if not entirely affectionately, as the "sweatbox"; and the closest thing the lot had to a cafeteria was the aptly named "Candy Closet."

Space was at a premium, to say the least. The stage at Hyperion was a "catch-all," accommodating sound recording, theater

A panoramic shot of the vacant Burbank lot prior to the start of construction (1939).

functions, rerecording, and any other activity that called for a large auditorium space. By necessity, the entire *Bambi* production unit was moved off the Hyperion lot to a facility several miles away at 861 Seward Street in Hollywood. The Story, Promotion, Engineering, Comic Strip, and Training departments were also relocated, to the second floor of 1717 North Vine Street in Hollywood.

A new, cohesively designed campus would allow the studio to recentralize its operation while also giving the various creative teams room to breathe. But Walt wasn't just looking for ample square footage; he wanted the new studio to clearly reflect the needs and preferences of his staff—from directors and animators to in-betweeners, inkers, and painters to cameramen—believing that ideal working conditions would create superior production and creativity.

In a move decades ahead of its time, Walt commissioned a detailed, collaborative study of the studio's needs before the plant was built. "We took the best ideas of all the fellows," recalled Frank Crowhurst, a structural engineer and architect assigned to the project. "I would sit and listen to animators and story men and different heads of departments—Dave Hand, Ham Luske, Perce Pearce, [Norm] Ferguson—[with] Walt being the voice most of the time. But the things arrived at there were the things we did, and it has been shown that they were very practical."

Walt envisioned an idyllic, parklike campus, not unlike the well-manicured grounds of surrounding universities. "The whole scheme has been laid out with two main ideas," Crowhurst explained while the lot was getting ready. "That it should not be, nor have, the appearance of being an industrial plant; that it should be broad in its scope and that none of the buildings should be too high, so that the streets would have a general campus feeling . . . When this place is all finished and landscaped, it will have a very magnificent feeling about it. You go over to any motion-picture lot and you will find a street twenty feet wide so trucks can get about, and buildings fifty or sixty feet high. They are long alleyways."

Early Burbank studio construction—Walt, Bill Garity (second from the right), and visitors in front of the new Animation Building (October 20, 1939).

Photo of Bill Garity's wood model of the new Burbank studio, taken by Disney staff photographer Herman Schultheis in 1939.

Walt Disney in his Hyperion studio office, perusing Kem Weber's renderings of the planned front gate of the new Burbank studio (1939).

Ever the innovator, Walt wanted to marry function and design by creating a studio with the look and feel of "a miniature game preserve." A considered artificial brook might double as a flood-control device, as it runs through beautifully landscaped grounds where, Garity said, the two pet Disney deer, Bambi and Faline, and squirrel, chipmunk, rabbit, and turtle friends might frolic and play.

He also insisted on abundant creature comforts for the hardworking human inhabitants of his new plant as well. Plans were made for horseshoe courts, Ping-Pong tables, a volleyball court, a baseball field, expansive lawn areas for picnicking, wide walkways for afternoon strolls, rooftop sundecks, and ample

eating areas. Garity recalled Walt's plan to have "Mickey Mouse and Silly Symphony productions run continuously every noon so that every employee will be familiar with all of the studio products."

The original designs also called for Stage One—and all subsequent stages—to be convertible into badminton courts after hours and a regulation swimming pool that would double as a water tank for the studio's air-conditioning system to "save money and make the 850 employees happy at one fell swoop," Garity said. This idea, a "green" innovation well before the term was even coined, was eventually scrapped in favor of the studio's iconic covered water tower.

Groundbreaking of the new Walt Disney Studios in Burbank (1939).

A little cow grazes along a very sleepy Buena Vista Street (1939).

Construction begins with the foundation of a new studio restaurant (November 20, 1939).

Construction of the privacy berm surrounding the new Burbank studio lot (c. 1940).

At one point, there was even talk of putting up apartments on the lot for Walt's employees, according to artist Joe Grant. Animator Ward Kimball remembered a meeting with Walt during which a similar idea was discussed. "'We will build them kind of like *Snow White*-type cottages [across the street from the studio], and they will have kind of a Disney theme. The rent will be cheap,'" he recalled Walt saying.

But when Kimball took the idea back to his fellow artists, they all balked. Proximity to the studio would mean being on call around the clock and Walt was notorious for working late. The odds of this would only increase within the new studio, where Walt was designing an attached apartment space for himself.

On one point, however, Walt was steadfast: the new Burbank studio would avoid the mistake that doomed the Hyperion lot. Every building design for those on the new lot, according to Garity, had a contingency plan for future growth. The Animation Building, for example, could add extensions to the north side, while the Ink and Paint, Camera, and Cutting buildings might tack on wings to the back if and when the time came. (And indeed, both the Camera and Cutting buildings did expand years later.) Crowhurst added, "We have set these buildings on this particular piece of ground so that we can expand every department without ever sacrificing that feeling of spaciousness."

As Disney's visionary-in-chief, Walt took his

The Animation Building under construction (October 20, 1939).

The berm was initially built to screen the lot from view. Its wooded areas later provided background for live-action filming (c. 1940).

planning one step further. Television in 1939–1940 was a nascent, uncertain medium, yet Disney even then saw potential in it, nonetheless, as Crowhurst explained: "Walt has made the point that if television comes in, it might change the whole setup. And where would we be in that case? We might want a building as big as the Animation Building that would have to be planned entirely differently. Then it would be too bad if we had to sell everything and move to another lot. So that piece of ground is reserved for such a contingency, though nothing is contemplated at this time. In other words, Walt has tried to analyze every possible future contingency." Indeed, when the studio opened its doors in 1940, only 40 percent of the site was developed.

Garity was tapped to oversee the massive construction project, and he wasted no time in implementing Walt's vision. By December 1938, fourteen people were working on the new studio site: an architect, a builder, a technical engineer, a small crew of draftsmen, a telephone operator, and a secretary. "When they are not actively engaged in work pertaining to the new twenty-acre plant, they are either swatting flies or chasing neighboring cows off the property," he noted. "The cows, it seems, insist on looking upon the builders' wooden stakes in the ground as tempting *hors d'oeuvres.*"

As luck would have it, "hungry cows" were the only obstacle the construction project would have to endure. Only a year after placing a deposit down on the site, the new Walt Disney Studios in Burbank welcomed its first wave of employees.

Camera work on *Pinocchio* was started in the new Camera Building on August 24, 1939, and the *Bambi* unit moved into the still-incomplete Animation Building later that fall. The general move out of the Los Feliz facility and to Burbank took place between December 26, 1939, and January 5, 1940. "Over the Christmas holiday, we shut down for two weeks," recalled Roger Broggie, who worked in the studio Camera Department. "Everything was moved during the holiday, and then they opened up after New Year's."

The arrival of General Electric air-conditioning parts and motors on November 16, 1939.

BILL GARITY

Bill Garity, operating early studio sound equipment (1930s).

One of the unsung heroes of Disney, Bill Garity, helped Mickey Mouse find his voice in *Steamboat Willie* and thunderstruck audiences with *Fantasia*'s powerful score, among other innovations.

"With his pioneering efforts in sound and camera techniques, he helped set Disney Studios apart from others," said Dave Smith, founder and chief archivist of the Walt Disney Archives.

Born in Brooklyn, New York, on April 2, 1899, Bill attended the Pratt Institute in New York before serving with the radio research and development section of the U. S. Army Signal Corps during the First World War. He met radio pioneer Lee de Forest soon after the war and spent the next seven years helping develop early sound for film.

In 1927, Bill installed an audio system in New York's Capitol Theatre to accompany an exciting innovation in film: the first newsreel with sound. The reel featured footage of aviator Charles Lindbergh's reception in Washington, D.C., following his successful crossing of the Atlantic.

A year later, he met Walt while developing the Cinephone motion-picture recording system. Walt was so taken with the system that he hired Bill to record and engineer Steamboat Willie, the first cartoon to feature synchronized sound. The runaway success of that short convinced Walt to purchase the Cinephone system and "rent" Bill to install it out in California. But his sixty-day trip to the West Coast ended up lasting longer than Bill anticipated—by about thirteen years. Shortly after coming west, Garity was leading a team of eighteen skilled engineers who would help revolutionize the animated form.

Among his inventions: the multiplane camera, which allowed for camera movements that simulated live-action cinematography. First featured in the 1937 short, *The Old Mill*, the multiplane camera would be used to great effect in classics like *Pinocchio* and *Bambi*, and would even go on to earn an Academy Award in the Scientific and Technical Award category. Today, one of Bill's original multiplane cameras can be viewed just outside the Walt Disney Archives on the studio lot.

By 1934, Walt had appointed Bill as Disney's first production manager, and five years later he enlisted him to help design the new studio lot in Burbank. Once that mission was under way, Bill and his team refocused their energies on yet another innovation: Fantasound, a stereo system installed in theaters for Disney's animated classic, *Fantasia*. The stereo system greatly enhanced the effect of the musical masterpiece, which would earn an Academy Award nomination in 1941.

One year later, Bill left Disney to pursue other entertainment ventures, including a stint as vice president and production manager of Walter Lantz Studios. He died in Los Angeles on September 16, 1971, and was inducted posthumously as a Disney Legend in 1999.

Bill Garity works on designs for the new Burbank studio equipment (c. 1939).

The move happened fast so as not to interrupt the studio's breakneck production schedule. "All of the equipment [was moved]—test cameras, camera cranes. In fact, I shot right up until midnight, running three shifts," Broggie said. "I shut down at midnight. We struck the crane, moved it to Burbank, and we started up again at eight o'clock in the morning in Burbank. There were trucks hurtling back and forth. I think that was a big push, to get *Pinocchio* out."

The January 12, 1940, edition of *The Bulletin*, the studio's employee newsletter, posted an update in its "We Don't Know—We Only Heard" section: "Not only does this old deserted studio [the former one in Los Feliz] have the 'feel' of a ghost town, but at this writing it is beginning to take on the battered appearance of a city in ruins…There's still quite a few people here at that, bravely carrying on; Inking and Painting girls, looking quite forlorn, the business offices, casting, comic strip, publicity, story research, promotion[,] and stockroom are some of the departments holding the fort."

Quite a few of these departments wouldn't make the move to the new locale until spring, while over at the new Burbank plant, the Commissary opened on March 21, and the Studio Theater building followed on April 10. *The Bulletin* would continue to lightheartedly document the move from Los Feliz's Hyperion facility to Burbank throughout the first half of 1940, as in its "Inkers-Painters Move Monday" dispatch from May 3, 1940:

Woe-begone [sic] looks on the faces of several Disney males who have been desolate since they moved to Burbank away from the glances of the Inking and Painting department will no doubt disappear when the entire unit moves into their new building Monday.

New home of the girls, in addition to being completely air-conditioned, excellently lighted, and containing special lounge rooms, will have its own cafeteria, which will be operated solely for the benefit of the girls in this department. [Animator] Woolie [Reitherman] will just have to stay away—that's final.

The very last group to move to Burbank was the Sodium Process Laboratory, following the new lab's completion in October 1940. By then, according to *The Bulletin*'s report from September 13, even the chief contractor of Disney's new home had moved on.

VALLEY HOME OFFER

Frank Crowhurst, having just polished off construction supervision of the studio, is building a group of valley homes, it was announced this week.

Site is Ben Avenue, just north of Magnolia, total sales price per unit ranging under $5,000.

Homes are described as having living toom [sic] and den, each with fireplace, 2 bedrooms, dining alcove, kitchen, and bathroom. Lots are 58 feet wide.

Olympia 1 6 0 6 will catch Mr. Crowhurst.

Walt's new studio was finally complete.

Overhead view of the studio under construction, taken from the water tower on September 5, 1939.

Valley Progress magazine, featuring the soon-to-open Walt Disney Studios (October 1939).

The move onto the new Burbank lot began over the holidays, December 28, 1939.

Walt Disney admires the view from his new third-floor office in the Animation Building (October 20, 1939).

WALKING WALT'S STUDIO

The filming of conductor Leopold Stokowski's shadow for *Fantasia* on Stage One (1940).

Soon after the new Walt Disney Studios opened in 1940, Walt began taking his young children for visits, a tradition his eldest daughter, Diane Disney Miller, would recall fondly years later.

"It became our weekend playground," Miller said. "And it was a wonderful place. Dad would take us there on a Saturday or a Sunday afternoon. No one else was around. And he'd throw our bikes in the car. And it was all so new. And it was all ours."

Many of Disney's biggest stars also had a soft spot for the studio. Fess Parker, who played Davy Crockett, would remember it as "collegial and calm and peaceful. And the people were more like family than any place I'd been."

Mouseketeer Sharon Baird echoed this sentiment: "It was so pleasant to work there. I had worked at other studios. With the grass and the flowers and the names of the streets, everyone that worked at Disney was the most pleasant . . . everyone would say, 'Hi!' Just like talking to Mickey and Minnie every day. Just real up."

Such reactions were, of course, just what Walt had in mind while planning his new studio. He hired well-known German architect Karl Emanuel Martin Weber to design the site plan, as well as all the buildings and furnishings. Weber would describe his artistic philosophy in simple terms: "To make the practical more beautiful and the beautiful more practical."

As with every project Walt undertook, the studio design was a collaborative effort, according to Frank Crowhurst: "It is really a Disney plant. It isn't that Walt had anything against architects. He didn't. But he realized that if he gave one of them the job, he would have to move into the architect's building, and he didn't want to do that.

"He wanted his building," Crowhurst explained once the Burbank project was proceeding. "Instead of having any one architect or any one person here, it is like the way Disney Studio[s] makes pictures; Walt has insisted that everybody be in on the thing. Neither [Kem] Weber, Jim Lill, our head engineer, nor I have had a free hand in anything—or Walt himself. We have taken the collective thoughts of everyone and used the best that was offered."

The team pored over every element of the design plan, right down to the colors, which, as Walt knew from his animated movies, had the power to affect emotion and mood. He, Weber, and Crowhurst experimented with various shades and schemes on the Hyperion back lot. "We thought at that time we should get some sense of California colors or desert colors, or something that would be gay rather than the somberness of dark red brick," Crowhurst recalled. Eventually, the trio settled on the studio's trademark palette of green, red, and beige earth tones, colors that are incorporated into any new Disney buildings to this day.

The new studio front gate at 500 S. Buena Vista St. in Burbank (1940).

Walt Disney (left) and Kem Weber (center) look over plans for studio furniture construction at the Peterson Show Case & Fixture Company in Los Angeles (November 1939).

KEM WEBER

Kem Weber and Walt Disney inspect furniture construction at the Peterson Show Case & Fixture Company in Los Angeles (November 1939).

One of the founders of the influential art moderne style of architecture, Karl Emanuel Martin Weber, began his career building furniture.

As stated in *Kem Weber, The Moderne in Southern California 1920 Through 1941*, Weber was born in Germany in 1889 and entered the workshop of the royal cabinetmaker, Eduard Schulz, at age fifteen. After graduating in 1907, he attended the Royal Academy of Applied Arts, in Berlin, and studied under architect and designer Bruno Paul. Weber worked in Paul's private studio for two years before being recommended in 1914 to help design the German section of the 1915 Panama-Pacific International Exposition in San Francisco. He traveled to the city to oversee construction of the exhibit but was unable to return home when World War I broke out in Europe.

After spending a year as a chicken farmer, Weber established his own practice as a designer and architect, first in Santa Barbara, California, and later in Los Angeles. He married Erika Forke and became a U.S. citizen in 1924. By 1930, he was one of America's better-known industrial designers, in part for his work in the International Exposition of Art in Industry at Macy's department store in New York City. He also taught at the University of Southern California and The Art Center school (now the Art Center College of Design) before his death on January 31, 1963.

Best known for his iconic 1934 "Airline" chair, Weber's sensibility is reflected in the moderne approach in which, note David Gebhard and Harriette Von Breton, "sharp linear angularity of the total design is the dominant quality. Lines are used as a decorative motif. All decoration was purposefully repetitive. Surfaces tend to be plain, smooth, sleek, and simple."

Kem Weber watercolor rendering of office décor for the new Animation Building (1939).

Weber rendering of the exterior of the new Walt Disney Studios restaurant (1939).

Wide lawns and pedestrian thoroughfares—with trees and shrubbery similar to what grew in nearby Griffith Park—complemented the warm, inviting feeling that Walt sought. "The main thing is to get a stretch of lawn on each side of the roadway—our walk," Crowhurst said. "We don't allow vehicles. The roadways around the buildings are entirely reserved for walking. They are wide enough so they look like streets, but they are actually walks." Walt would later adopt this same concept for Main Street, U.S.A. in Disneyland (and the other parks have since followed suit).

All these steps had the intended results, even years later. Robert Loggia, star of the late 1950s Disney television show *The Nine Lives of Elfego Baca*, said, "When you were at the studio, it looked like a high school or college campus, [with] people playing volleyball and everyone on a first-name basis."

Today, the Burbank lot retains the same relaxing, parklike charm. Staffers and guests are regularly seen taking strolls, picnicking on the grass, or enjoying a meal on the outdoor patios or air-conditioned indoor seating areas of the commissary.

THE COMMISSARY

The March 21, 1940, opening of the commissary afforded busy staffers the chance to have a good meal without having to leave the friendly confines of the studio, an important perk given the dearth of lunch spots in 1940s Burbank. The facility was divided into two parts: "…a restaurant for those who want to linger over their dinner, and a coffee shop where they can be served quickly and where they can turn them over three times an hour," Crowhurst said.

The first, temporary commissary at the new studio was actually a soundstage, according to the January 12, 1940, *Bulletin*:

A complete restaurant, [with] even flowers on the tables, has been laid out in the Live Action Stage on the Burbank lot and is being operated by the Brittingham Commissary. This has been done for the comfort and convenience of the employees[,] and everyone is invited to take advantage of its excellent facilities.

This restaurant came into being over last weekend, with carpenters, painters, plumbers[,] and electricians working night and day to complete the setup for Monday's lunch.

The Brittingham Commissary is to be complimented on the fine food and service. Both a cafeteria and dining room have been installed. A full-course luncheon in the dining room may be had for 60¢—the same luncheon is 50¢ in the cafeteria. Sandwiches and salads are offered at popular prices, pies and desserts are 10¢[,] and coffee is a nickel.

In order to provide the best possible facilities and insure that only the highest quality food is served, the studio pays a flat rate of 80¢ for each person served, regardless of the amount of the check.

The "Cartoon Special," on the menu daily, is a particular feature. This consists of an entrée, rolls and butter, coffee, milk, or buttermilk, and is offered at 35¢ in the cafeteria, and 40¢ in the dining room.

The makeshift restaurant's promise of FINE FOOD AT POPULAR PRICES served to whet staffers' appetites for the new, permanent commissary. Within days of its opening, the commissary pushed back its opening time to 7:30 a.m. "in order that Disneyites may enjoy a leisurely breakfast before starting work," according to the April 2 *Bulletin*:

The Assistant Directors meet regularly for breakfast on Friday mornings, and it is hoped that other groups in the studio will take advantage of the facilities offered. Victor [Bronnais the commissary manager] will be glad to arrange special parties at any time, so if you have a birthday celebration . . . give him a ring.

It is the hope of the restaurant management to see Disney employees using the restaurant for all their parties, so ask your friends over to lunch anytime, and have your wives or girlfriends over for dinner.

Victor's invitation for staffers to invite guests sparked a good-natured brouhaha. One cheeky "Disneyite" submitted a letter in the April 19 issue of *The Bulletin* that ran with the headline, "VICTOR HEARS FROM VOCAL STOMACH."

[Your invitation] is a very lovely thought, but not at all practical. There is a very efficient police system just for the purpose of keeping all those people out of the Studio [sic]. Of course, I could use a parachute to drop my friends on the roof of your charming restaurant, but I have so many friends that, the price of parachutes being what it is, it might develop into a rather expensive proposition. I even thought of disguising them as traffic boys and walking them through the gates, but there was always the danger of them protruding where they should not intrude.

One of the boys here even thought of smuggling in his girl in one of your luxurious 'residuum' cans, but that won't work either. At the exit gate everything goes out; nothing comes in!

So, if you can tear yourself away from your potages and fillets long enough to give this matter consideration, enlighten us via *The Bulletin*. Meanwhile, rather than incur the displeasure of the Gate Gestapo, we'll eat alone and like it.

Coffee shop dining area of the new Walt Disney's Studio Restaurant (1940).

Walt and Alexander P. de Seversky have lunch at Walt's table in the Studio Restaurant executive dining room—the "Coral Room"—during production of *Victory Through Air Power* (in 1942).

Cover of the first Walt Disney's Studio Restaurant daily menu (1940).

Cover of the first Studio Restaurant breakfast menu (1940).

First Studio Restaurant daily menu (1940).

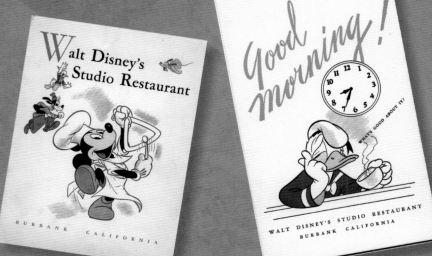

Not to be outdone, Victor would respond in kind:

Dear Stomach:

This seems a very intimate form of address, but you leave me no choice.

The mere thought of your friends dropping in via parachute sends cold chills running up and down my spine, as they would more than likely land on one of our kitchen skylights and thence into the 60 gallon stock kettle. So in order to save ourselves the bother of straining the soup for your friends, I hired myself to the Personnel

Dept, where Hugh Pressly assured me that he will be glad to issue passes for your friends at any time you want to ask them to lunch. It will not be necessary for you to have a pass for dinner parties—just show your own identification card at the gate, and you will be admitted.

As for smuggling the girl friend [sic] in by the "residuum" can route, I feel sure this would lead to complications—what with the hats the girls wear nowadays. However, you are wrong about everything going out the gate, and nothing coming in. Drop around some morning and see the loads of meat, eggs, fruits, vegetables, and the thousand and one other things we use every day.

I trust this will serve to assure you that your friends are welcome at the Studio [sic] restaurant at any time, and that this department remains:

Obediently yours,
Victor Bronnais

With all the critical kinks now ironed out, the commissary became a vital hub at the new studio, a place to dine and, just as importantly, to see and be seen. Most Disneyites frequented the restaurant, including Walt himself. According to Kathryn Beaumont, the voice of Alice from

Alice in Wonderland and Wendy from *Peter Pan*, "Walt was a person who was quite visible. Most studio heads, I had learned, you know . . . they're in an office somewhere. But, Walt would come down to the cafeteria and go through the line at lunchtime, with his tray, and find a place to sit just as everybody else was doing at lunch. He would visit with people."

During one of her frequent visits to the studio to meet with Walt, renowned Hollywood gossip columnist Hedda Hopper noted, in June 1963, "A small boy was playing Ping-Pong. A little boy with a yellow necktie and yellow socks was playing around outside the entrance to the dining room. Walt said, 'Hello, Matthew. How are you?' and as he passed patted him on the head. The little boy glowed." Hopper's visit took place during production of *Mary Poppins*; the little boy on his lunch break was Matthew Garber, who played young Michael Banks.

Moments later, as the columnist recounted, "Julie Andrews came by in a pert little hat with a daisy sticking up in front. Walt said, 'I'm gonna give you that when the picture's done,' referring to Mary Poppins'[s] signature hat. Julie replied, 'I want it so badly and didn't want to ask.'"

Staff members enjoy games of Ping-Pong on the commissary deck (c. 1946).

Disney artists enjoy a sunbath on the roof of the Animation Building (1940).

Staff dance party in front of the Animation Building (1946).

THE ANIMATION BUILDING

Just across Mickey Mouse Boulevard lay the crown jewel of Walt's new studio. It was the Animation Building, which housed his immensely talented staff of artists and animators—including the legendary "Nine Old Men," as well as other artists like Herb Ryman and Joe Grant—songwriters like the Sherman brothers (starting in the 1950s), and, of course, from the beginning, Walt and his brother Roy O. It was, in many ways, the beating heart of the growing

Disney empire; virtually every production, from animated films to live-action movies, to theme park projects to television shows, was conceived within these walls.

Animator Glen Keane, who would draw such classic Disney characters as Ariel, Beast, Aladdin, and Pocahontas, recalled his first day on the job at the Burbank property in 1974: "I walked into that Animation Building . . . and it was not real bright in there," Keane said during a 1999 interview with Disney historian John

South entrance of the Animation Building (1973).

Directing Animator Woolie Reitherman drawing Timothy Mouse for *Dumbo* (1941).

Walt and animation staff work on *Alice in Wonderland* (1951). Left to right: Eric Larson, Walt Disney, Ken O'Connor, and Hamilton Luske.

Canemaker. "You could almost smell and feel the history that had gone on before. It was just really heavy or charged with history for me.

"I felt like I did as an altar boy and you're going back into where the priest gets dressed before he goes out and says Mass, and you smell the incense. Except there, it was a different kind of smell, the smell of pencil shavings and animation drawings. There was something magical about it, and I felt completely unworthy to be there."

The building's physical layout was meant to mirror and in fact streamline, the development process of Disney's animated features. "We have tried to set up our structure as to meet the requirements of the minimum amount of waste in time, effort, and movement," Bill Garity explained as staff was moving in. This "top-down" design began, of course, with Walt's third-floor suite. He shared the floor with his various story teams . . . the easier to keep a close eye on all projects in the studio pipeline.

The second floor, meanwhile, housed the offices of each of the film's director, layout men, and background artists. The first floor was for animation. Studio Manager Bill Garity estimated that 90 percent of the offices, home to Walt's famed animators, were filled by men. Two notable exceptions: Retta Scott, the first female animator at Disney, and famed color stylist and artist Mary Blair, both of whom began working at the studio in the 1940s.

Test cameras were set up in the basement, allowing the production teams to quickly evaluate their work without having to visit the always-busy Camera Department across the street. The basement also housed the studio morgue, from which staffers often pulled reference materials from past productions.

Walt also made sure to spoil his hardworking creative teams with generous amenities. "When [Walt] built this studio . . . [well] it's fantastic what he put in here. No one has ever had it as good," Animator (and one of Disney's legendary Nine Old Men) Frank Thomas gushed. "You could pick up your phone so you didn't have to leave your desk and say, 'I want a chocolate milk shake.' And as soon as you'd hang up, someone would come in with the chocolate milk shake."

If the artists wanted to stretch their legs, they could pop down to the building's first-floor coffee shop for a break . . . at least initially. Animator Ollie Johnston, another member of the Nine Old Men, recalled, "A lot of guys were sitting at that snack bar all day long and Walt would see them there every time he went by, and he finally closed it down."

The Animation Building's ultimate amenity was its exclusive "Penthouse Club," featuring a fully equipped gymnasium, steam and massage room, a barbershop, and dining rooms. A product of its time, the club did not allow female members and at one point had a rooftop sundeck where the animators could sunbathe *au naturel*.

This practice quickly fell out of fashion when the multistory St. Joseph's Hospital was built across Buena Vista Street and Mother Superior learned that her nuns were spying on the men.

ACROSS MINNIE AVENUE AND DOPEY DRIVE

Across the street from the Animation Building, the studio's critically important technical departments—Ink and Paint, Camera, and Cutting—had two buildings of their own.

In designing the Ink and Paint space, Walt and his team sought to fix the flaws of its Hyperion Avenue-based predecessor, which was, according to Frank Crowhurst, "totally inadequate" in virtually every respect. The new building was, for starters, two and a half times larger and built with three considerations in mind: light, cleanliness, and comfort. It boasted large banks of north-facing windows, offering the color stylists and painters the best possible conditions for selecting and applying color to the animation drawings. This was no middling concern given the Paint Laboratory's catalog contained more than two thousand different colors from the studio's many features and shorts.

"The provision of pure north light for each of the eight work corridors necessitated the leaving open of areas between alternate pairs of corridors," said Garity. "These areas have been utilized to provide pleasant landscaping and flower beds, which lend a friendly aspect to all rooms which open to them." The large patio

"areas"—appropriately named The Inkwell and The Paintwell—were popular features regularly enjoyed by the staff for lunches and breaks; and they still are today.

Cleanliness had also been a constant challenge at the Hyperion site, since even a speck of dust on an animation cel would result in a noticeable blemish on-screen. Therefore, the new building was fitted with linoleum floors and "lint-less interiors," which meant no carpets or draperies of any kind. Staff wore white lab coats over their clothes. Walt even built an underground tunnel between the Ink and Paint and Animation buildings to eliminate the risk of rain, wind, and dust damaging cels during the short stroll across Minnie Avenue, according to Garity.

As with the Animation Building, Walt balanced his concern for efficiency with a desire to keep his staff happy. The Ink and Paint Building, comprised mostly of women, offered the same amenities as its male-centric counterpart, with a lounge, private restaurant, and sundeck. "The girls have a very, very fine lounge there, too, so they can lie down. It is almost a club room, in a way, in as much as it is entirely reserved for them," Crowhurst explained when the structure was finished. Given the largely segregated amenities at the studio, it is no wonder that the male staff jokingly referred to the Ink and Paint Building as "The Nunnery."

A corridor connected Ink and Paint to the nearby Camera and Cutting buildings, once again to protect animation cels and other production

continued on page 46

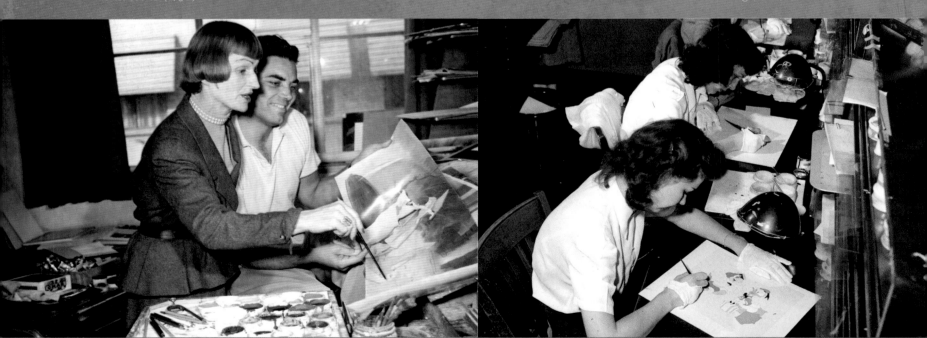

Artists Mary Blair and Claude Coats go over layouts for *Cinderella* (1950).

Studio inkers hard at work on cels for *Fantasia*, in their new facilities in the Ink and Paint Building (1940).

Painting stations in the new Ink and Paint Department (1940).

Walt Disney's desk in the northeast corner of his formal office, Animation Building Suite 3H5 (1970).

WALT DISNEY'S OFFICE

Every Sunday evening beginning in 1955, Walt would welcome the American public into his cozy office as part of ABC's hour-long Disneyland anthology program. There, "Uncle Walt" might share details about the progress of his magical new theme park or introduce the latest episode of serialized shows like *Davy Crockett*.

Walt's "office" was in actuality a production set tucked away on one of the studio's soundstages. His real headquarters was a ten-room suite located in H Wing on the third floor of the Animation Building. The space, which he designed himself, was surprisingly modest, with a receptionist area, two small secretarial offices, and separate public and private offices for Walt himself.

As studio chief, Disney understood the highly visible nature of his role. His formal office—set at the northeast corner of the suite—was decorated with awards, photos, and drawings of his daughters and grandchildren and mementos such as signed books by the likes of C. S. Lewis, Richard Nixon, and P. L. Travers that might interest visiting dignitaries and VIPs.

During her June 1963 visit to the studio, columnist Hedda Hopper noted, "Everywhere you look are figurines of Disney characters, medals of every size and inscription, plaques, [and] an original Norman Rockwell *Saturday Evening Post* cover on the wall in the hall. Two enchanting paintings of Mexican children were leaning against a sofa—a gift from the President [sic] of Mexico. The Japanese had evidently been there in droves bearing gifts—exquisite Japanese dolls were everywhere and some figures [were] done in something like porcelain. [Walt] pointed out gifts from Norway—pottery, a special sculpture done for him by the San Francisco art museum, a lion from Venice, and a trophy from Italy."

The furnishings of the formal office—stylish wood desk, a couch, chairs, various tables, and a baby grand piano—were uniquely designed for Walt by Kem Weber. Walt did not play the piano, but visiting musicians sometimes would, including *Fantasia* conductor Leopold Stokowski. The

A meeting in Walt Disney's working office. Left to right: Card Walker, Walt Disney, Harry Tytle, Bill Walsh (1958).

Sherman brothers frequently dropped by as well to play part of a new piece they were composing. Often, on Friday evenings, he would quietly ask Richard to play, and the songwriter would oblige with Walt's favorite number, "Feed the Birds" from *Mary Poppins*.

The smaller private office, where Disney and various members of the team did the serious business of creating make-believe, contained few such frills. Upon founding the Walt Disney Archives in 1970, Dave Smith first inventoried everything in the office suite, which had remained untouched since Walt's passing in 1966. "The thing that impressed me early on was that they were not elaborate offices that you would expect of the head of a company this big," Smith said. "Most of the furnishings were probably original—thirty years later they hadn't changed. So Walt obviously didn't need to impress people with his office. And it struck me that this was just a very friendly area, a very comfortable area to be in, like putting on a pair of old slippers. I'd seen photographs of offices of other studio heads like Louis B. Mayer and Jack Warner, and you come in the door and you walk yards and yards across this long carpet to get to the desk. Walt's office wasn't like that at all."

Thelma "Tommie" Wilck, one of Walt's secretaries from 1958 through 1966, described her boss at work: "When Walt was through meeting with people, he worked on scripts at his desk," she said. " He was in at eight-thirty in the morning, and he went home at seven or seven-thirty at night—and it was a long, busy day. There was somebody in his office every day, having meetings. If he was in his office, he was working. . . . The office door was always open. He never closed the office, and he had fantastic powers of concentration."

Wilck also recalled Walt's sometimes volatile temperament: "During the first year I was up in his office, there were times when he wore what we called his 'wounded bear suit,' when he was just meaner than poison. This particular time, he'd been wearing his wounded bear suit for several days and I was, frankly, getting a little fed up with it. He had called me on something I had already told him about earlier in the day.

"I said something like, 'As I told you this morning . . .' And he said, 'You don't need to be so damned sassy about it!' He was furious. With that he got up from his desk, walked over to the door, turned around, and said, 'You don't have to work here. There are other places where you can go.'

"I took that to mean he fired me. By this time I was crying, I was so mad. So I gathered up all the stuff from my desk. When he came back, he went to his desk and called me to come in. He never said he was sorry. He just said I didn't need to look for another job and added, 'But, you were sassy!'"

Given his hectic schedule, Walt built some creature comforts into his private office, including a kitchenette hidden behind a sliding wall. He also added a small adjoining bedroom and bathroom, though he'd only stayed overnight when deadlines were looming. The room was more commonly used for massage therapy treatments that studio nurse Hazel George would administer to control Walt's chronic pain, the result of a polo accident in his younger days.

Hopper, in her notes describing the private office, also recounted a surprising moment of insight into Walt's moviemaking philosophy: "He calls the smaller room his workshop. Photographs of his family are very much in evidence," she wrote. "Beside him he has a large chart that listed all his pictures and give their domestic, foreign[,] and total gross. He pointed to a couple— *Swiss Family Robinson* that did $7,850,000 domestic and $3,700,000 foreign to date, and *Parent Trap*— $12,750,000 total and *Absent-Minded Professor*—$12,050,000 and said, 'The critics didn't care for these pictures. I ignore the critics.

"'But I do believe Hollywood is influenced by them—the profession is influenced by them. The key is the audience. If a certain critic praises one of our films, I get worried. I think pictures should be made in spite of the critics. My barometer is public acceptance.'"

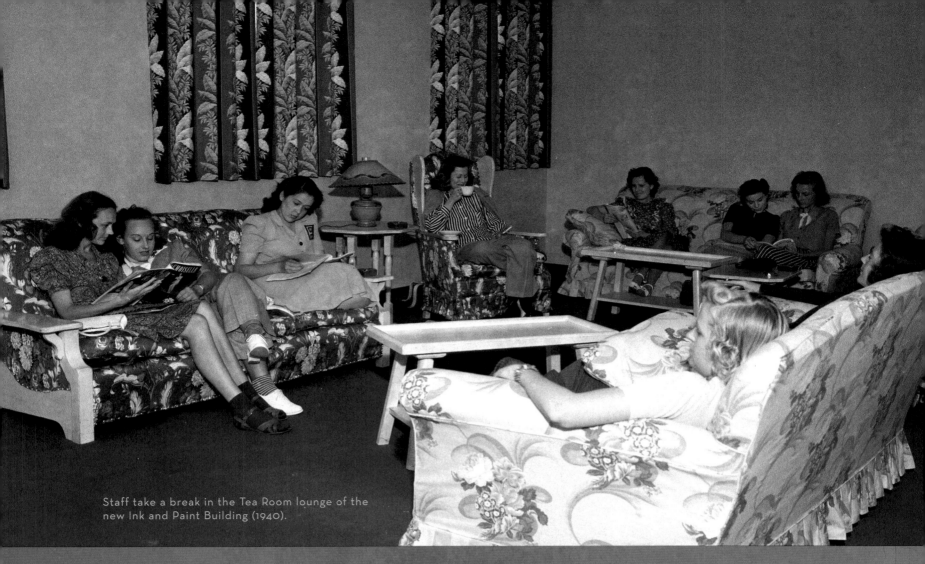

Staff take a break in the Tea Room lounge of the new Ink and Paint Building (1940).

materials from exposure to the outdoor elements. A unique feature within the Camera Building took this concern one step further. All personnel entering the camera rooms passed through a special de-dusting chamber in which twenty separate nozzles blasted air at high velocity to remove lint and dust. An even more impressive innovation was housed inside: two gigantic multiplane cameras. This groundbreaking camera technology, designed and built by Garity, added rich layers of depth and perspective to Disney animated productions.

At the far end of the corridor was the Cutting Building, where picture and sound came together in the editing process. It served as the final stop before a movie's release in theaters. The building was entirely fireproof and airtight, a necessary precaution given the volatile nature of the explosive nitrate films used at this time.

Directly behind Cutting sat the studio's film vaults, a cluster of oddly shaped buildings, which were demolished in 2014. The vaults were uniquely designed so that if the nitrate film

stored inside exploded, the force of it would move upwards, blowing off their ceilings. As fire standards—thankfully—improved, the vaults were deemed insufficient for nitrate storage; the original film reels were put under the care of the Library of Congress in the early 1990s.

Along Dopey (originally Donald) Drive sat the studio's new, state-of-the-art Theater and Orchestra buildings, which Walt and his team designed themselves, according to Crowhurst. Boasting outstanding acoustics, the theater was used both to screen new films and as a "closed set" for sound mixing.

"The Theater and the Orchestra stage are the very last word in engineering design," Crowhurst said. "Nobody has an orchestra stage as fine as ours from the standpoint of recording music." From *Bambi* to *Bedknobs and Broomsticks*, the Orchestra Building (later known as Stage A) has been home to the maestros, musicians, and vocalists who brought the auditory magic to the Disney motion-picture experience. Today, music is recorded off-lot, and Stage A serves as an all-digital, cutting-edge dubbing facility.

Just east of the studio's Theater Building lay Stage B and Stage C. Stage B, commonly called the "Dialogue Stage," was actually a building within a building. Given the studio's proximity to the Burbank airport now known as Bob Hope Airport, the outer structure was built completely independent of the inner space so as to block background sounds from the stage's highly sensitive recording equipment. Character voices from animated films like *Alice in Wonderland*, *Lady and the Tramp*, and *The Jungle Book* to more contemporary classics such as *The Hunchback of Notre Dame*, *Toy Story*, *a bug's life*, and *Monsters, Inc.* have been recorded here.

Stage C was home to sound-effects wizard Jimmy Macdonald, who also served as the voice of Mickey Mouse starting in 1946 when Walt became too busy. Macdonald and his innovative team recorded sound effects for all animated films and shorts starting in 1940, using a variety of tools, including a ten-foot-deep water tank for realistic water-effects sounds. Today Stage C is a dubbing stage used for final mixing of film and video sound.

THE HYPERION BUILDINGS

In order to achieve the maximum amount of office space needed in Burbank, while remaining budget-conscious, Walt decided that it was necessary to transport some of the Hyperion studio buildings to the new Burbank location. In fact, Walt had six buildings moved in all.

One of the most noteworthy of these structures is the Shorts Building. The building actually consists of two separate wings of the Hyperion animation building, which were constructed in 1934 and 1937. The two wings were quite historic, and perhaps sentimental to Walt, as they housed animation units for early shorts, such as Mickey's first color cartoon (*The Band Concert*), Donald Duck's debut short (*The Wise Little Hen*), and hundreds of others, as well as the animation team for *Snow White and the Seven Dwarfs*. The buildings moved from Los Feliz in 1939 and upon arrival in Burbank, positioned together forming a "T."

In its new location, the Shorts Building housed the Comic Strip, Publicity, and Foreign departments. Years later, when the studio grew its live-action film production unit, it became the location for the Wardrobe, Makeup, and Music departments. More recently, the building has

The Hyperion Bungalow, which was moved to the Burbank lot in 1939, was used for various departments on the new lot over the years.

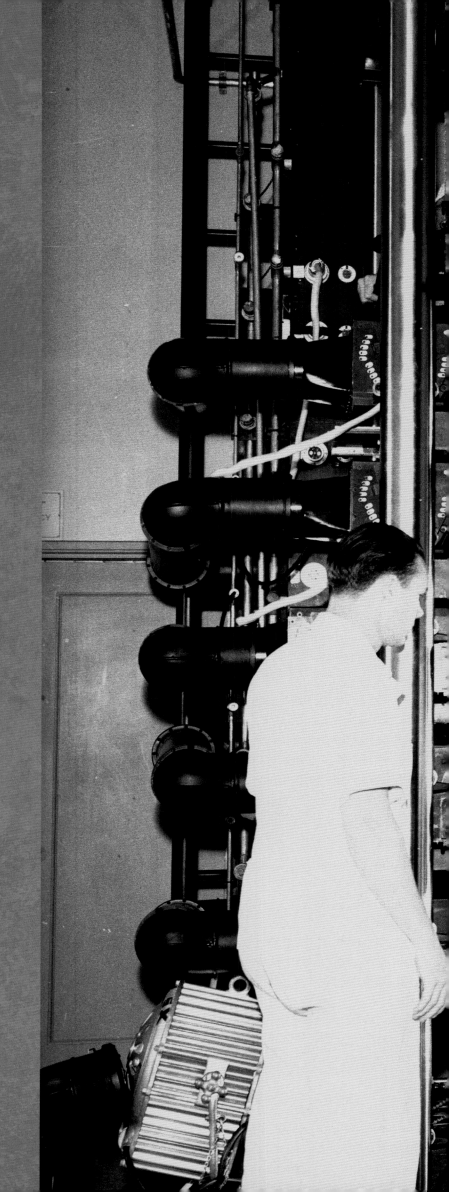

been completely restored and currently houses production offices to support live-action filming on the lot.

The Art Annex Building was originally situated across the street from the Hyperion studio. After being transported to Burbank, it was used as the studio's Personnel Building. Today it houses the studio's Disney Store, Employee Center, and the studio nurse.

Another historic building that moved to the Burbank studio is known as the Hyperion Bungalow. It was built in 1932 and was originally home to the Disney Comic Strip department. Once in Burbank, it was situated next to the commissary and housed Payroll, Publicity support, Traffic, and was finally the Studio Post Office and Employee Center. In 1995, it was moved across Mickey Avenue adjacent to the Disney Store, where it was renovated and converted into two conference rooms. The Hyperion Bungalow is the last remaining example of "California Bungalow"-type architecture from the Hyperion studio.

THE T.E.A.M. BUILDING

A short walk from the Animation Building, just behind Ink and Paint, resides the T.E.A.M. (Technical Engineering and Manufacturing) Building, which was constructed in early 1955.

Disney engineers designed, built, and maintained their huge animation production cameras in this building. Walt also used the site to indulge in his train hobby, tinkering with the machinists and building the engine and cars for his own backyard railroad line, the Carolwood Pacific Railroad, which was named for the street in the Holmby Hills area of Los Angeles where Walt and his family lived.

T.E.A.M. began as a manufacturing facility and machine shop during the peak of Disneyland's development. Many of the park's vehicles—automobiles, boats, trams, even the *Monorail*—were designed and built here, entirely by hand. Walt and his team also developed Disney's *Audio-Animatronics* for attractions like *Great Moments with Mr. Lincoln* and "it's a small world" in this building. As such, the structure is widely regarded as the birthplace of Walt

48

The multiplane camera in operation during the production of *Fantasia* (1940).

The "Dog Pound Quartet" sequence of *Lady and the Tramp* (1955).

The Mello-Men provide vocals for the "Dog Pound Quartet" in *Lady and the Tramp* (1955).

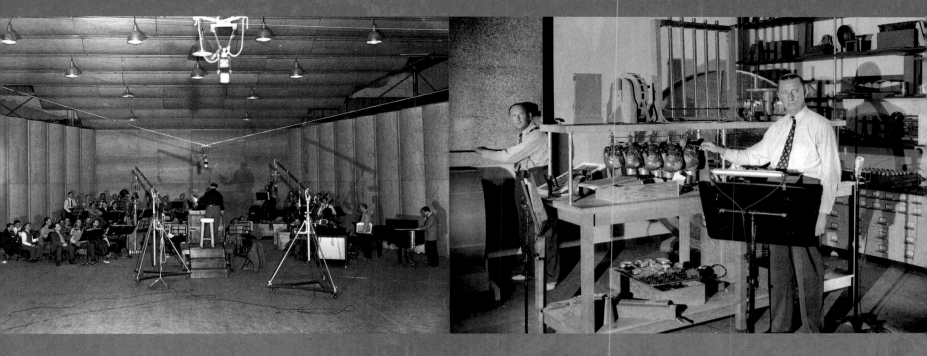

Orchestral recording of *Bambi* on Stage A. Center: Alexander Steinert. Right: Frederick Stark (copyist). Far right (at piano): Charles Wolcott (1942).

Sound effects recording on Stage C for *The Reluctant Dragon* by a Disney Foley artist (1940).

Disney Imagineering, the division that develops rides and attractions for Disney theme parks. When Imagineering moved to larger facilities in nearby Glendale, California, the studio renovated the T.E.A.M. Building and turned it into office space for its new mainstream record label, Hollywood Records.

SOUNDSTAGES

The only large-scale soundstage built as part of Walt's original Burbank studio was Stage One. Among the first projects filmed on the stage were the Leopold Stokowski interstitial segments of *Fantasia*. During World War II, Stage One was commandeered by the military, as was the entire studio, and was used for repairing armed forces trucks and antiaircraft equipment. As a national security measure, all studio cameras were cleared from the stage prior to military occupation, so there was no Disney motion-picture activity whatsoever during that period.

Stage Two was added in 1949 and was built in cooperation with Jack Webb, who was looking for a location to film his popular television cop drama, *Dragnet*. Other early productions filmed on Stage Two were Walt's first forays into the medium of television: *One Hour in Wonderland* (1950) and *The Walt Disney Christmas Show* (1951). Stage Two was also the primary shooting stage for Julie Andrews and Dick Van Dyke for Walt Disney's musical masterpiece, *Mary Poppins*. On August 2, 2001, both stars

Sound effects recording on Stage C (1940).

Construction of Stage Two (1947).

returned to Stage Two—alongside Mickey Mouse, the Disneyland Band, and a host of their "Jolly Holiday" penguin costars—when it was rededicated as The Julie Andrews Stage.

In 1954, Stage Three was constructed to satisfy the production demands for one of Walt Disney's most ambitious motion pictures to date, *20,000 Leagues Under the Sea*. The stage featured a unique water-effects tank that was divided into two parts. One tank was rather deep, while the other was shallow. There was a specially designed camera pit with three photographic ports and three viewing ports at varying levels so that both camera and crew could view and capture the action with the utmost flexibility. Of course, the tank was also equipped with a heater to ensure the comfort of Walt's stars. The climactic giant squid attack scene from *20,000 Leagues*, where Captain Nemo (James Mason) and Ned Land (Kirk Douglas) did battle with the fierce sea creature while standing on the deck of the *Nautilus*, was shot on this stage.

The final building added to Walt's studio during his lifetime was Stage Four in 1958. The first production filmed on the new stage was *Darby O'Gill and the Little People*, which required special lighting to achieve the film's special effects photography. To properly film the forced perspective of the leprechauns' throne room, huge sets had to be built and lit by numerous banks of lights. As a result, the stage was built with special ventilation to provide relief from the intense heat generated by the lighting.

Tron, a special effects tour de force and one of the first films to make significant use of computer-generated imagery (CGI), was shot on Stage Four in the early 1980s. By the mid-1980s, the studio had launched Touchstone Pictures to make more adult-oriented motion pictures, which significantly increased Disney's film output. One of the early films produced under the Touchstone banner was *Down and Out in Beverly Hills*, which marked a return to stardom for actors Richard Dreyfuss, Bette Midler, and Nick Nolte. The interiors of the Whiteman mansion—the estate of Dreyfuss and Midler's characters—were filmed on Stage Four.

Burbank Studio Machine Shop (1958).

Back lot standing sets first used in *Zorro* were later redressed for the movie *Monkeys, Go Home!* (1967).

THE STUDIO BACK LOT

Walt Disney's significant investment in television production gave birth to the studio's historic back lot.

The first permanent facades were built in 1957 for the new *Zorro* television series starring Guy Williams. In the show's first year, the sets were designed to appear as early 1800s Pueblo de Los Angeles; their versatility allowed them to be altered slightly to represent the Old Spanish central California town of Monterey during *Zorro's* second season.

A few years later the sets were being used in both movie and TV productions. They were a Provence, France-based village for 1967's *Monkeys, Go Home!* and an Italian village for the two-part television show *The Treasure of San Bosco Reef* (which aired as part of *Walt Disney's Wonderful World of Color*). And they made an appearance in the 1977 movie *Herbie Goes to Monte Carlo* with Dean Jones and Don Knotts.

Winding past the onetime *Zorro* sets would lead to the back lot's Western Street, most of which was constructed in 1958 for both *The Nine Lives of Elfego Baca* and *Texas John Slaughter* television series. The section featured transplants from several Disney productions, including a large two-story building that was built for *Darby O'Gill and the Little People*, a firehouse that was built in 1968 for *The Love Bug*, and the opera house and bank from *The Apple Dumpling Gang*. The last Disney features to use Western Street were *Hot Lead and Cold Feet* and *The Apple Dumpling Gang Rides Again*.

North of Western Street was Residential Street, whose four original buildings were constructed in 1960 for *The Absent-Minded Professor* and featured Ned Brainard's (Fred MacMurray) house and the garage laboratory where he invented "Flubber." Three more residential facades were added and later appeared in films like *Summer Magic* and 1965's *That Darn Cat*, and even the television show *The Swamp Fox*, starring Leslie Nielsen.

Walt gives a tour of the back lot to the daughters of actor
Ken Murray (1962).

Business Street was adjacent to Residential Street and features a charming town square with storefronts that were convertible to any period or locale. This versatile area of the back lot saw extensive use in Disney films and television series, including *The Ugly Dachshund*; *Follow Me, Boys!*; *That Darn Cat*; *The Happiest Millionaire*; *Charley and the Angel*; *Kilroy*; *Atta Girl, Kelly!*; and *The Shaggy D.A.* In 1981, the sets were demolished to make way for *Something Wicked This Way Comes*. The area was also used for the television series *Wildside*; a Dolly Parton special; and, of course, Disney-MGM Studios' *Muppet*Vision 3-D*, the last Muppets production Jim Henson produced before his death.

The new Burbank studio fulfilled Walt's vision completely, an ultramodern movie lot with the feel of an idyllic small town. Freed from the cramped confines of the Hyperion site, the Walt Disney Studios now had a home capable of realizing even the wildest dreams of its world's master storyteller. A sense of renewed optimism and pride abounded as excited staffers got back to the business of making movies, unaware that rising tensions outside the studio gates would soon bring war literally to Disney's doorstep.

Disney Studios back lot with its famous water tower, mill buildings, and the corner of Stage Three (1958).

1940'S LAYOUT OF STUDIO PLANT

1 - Walt Disney
2 - Story department
3 - Director
4 - Layout
5 - Background
6 - Animation
7 - Orchestra recording
8 - Sound effects recording
9 - Dialogue recording
10 - Inking and painting
11 - Camera
12 - Cutting
13 - Publicity - Public relations
14 - Live action stage
15 - Theatre
16 - Maintenance
17 - Process Lab.
18 - Central heating

A 1944 layout of studio plant showing the animation process. Note: No. 8 was the special effects offices, not recording as is listed in this layout.

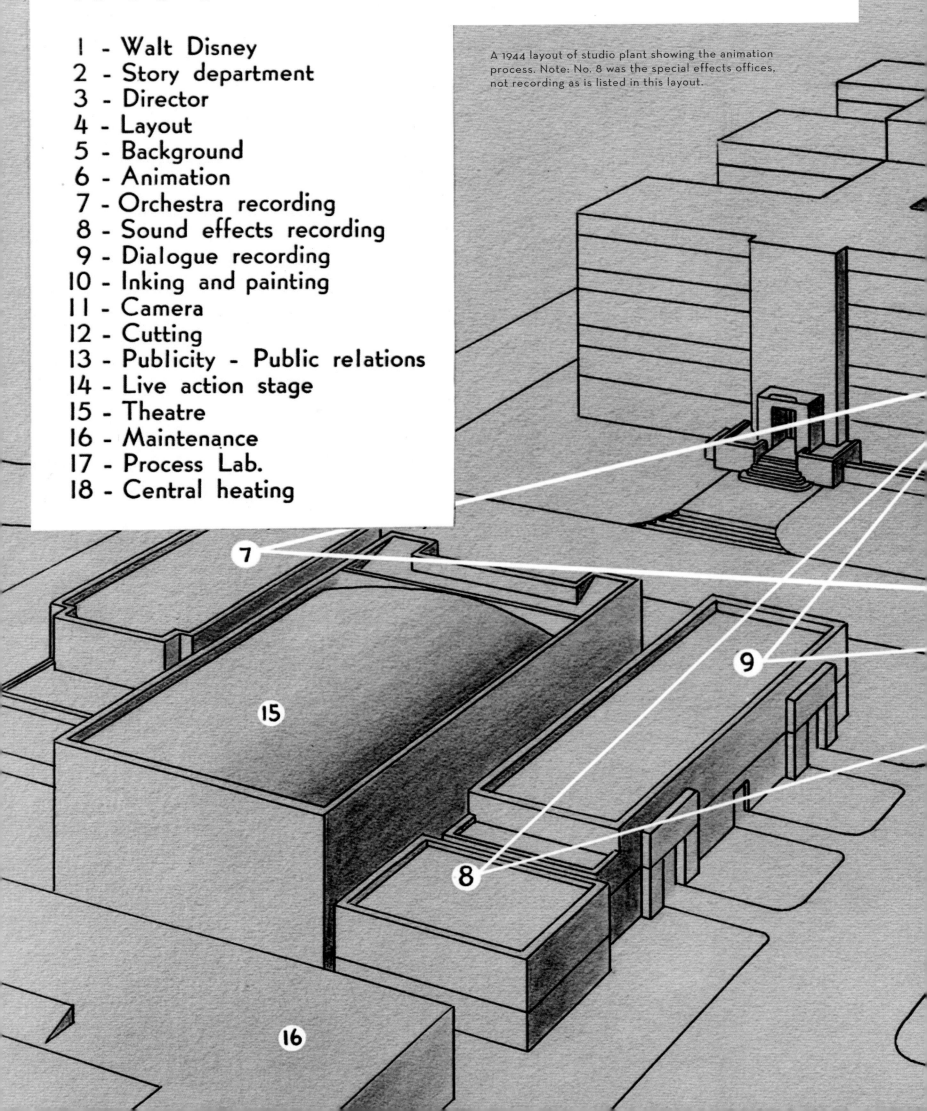

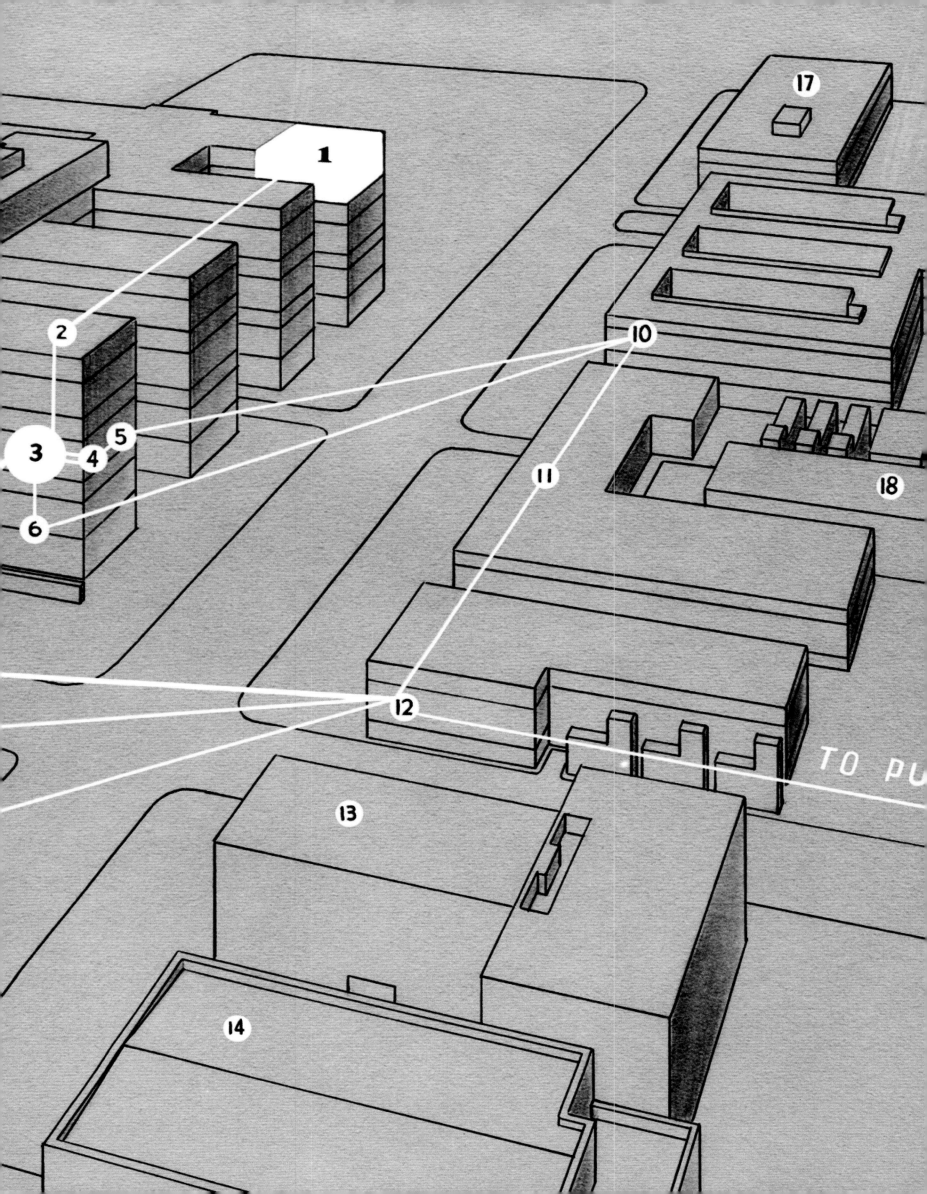

CHAPTER
4

STORM CLOUDS GATHER

U.S. Navy and Disney Studio staff work together
on a story for a new military short (1942).

With *Snow White and the Seven Dwarfs* filling the coffers and the staff of a newly opened dream studio already hard at work on new projects, the Walt Disney Studios seemed poised for even greater success as the 1930s wound down to a close. But the escalating conflict in Europe—and new internal challenges—would soon threaten not only the company's prosperity but its very existence.

On September 1, 1939, Adolf Hitler's Germany invaded Poland, effectively beginning the Second World War. The war sealed off overseas revenue, which by this time accounted for 45 percent of the studio's income. Germany, Italy, Poland, Austria, and Czechoslovakia were completely blocked from engaging in foreign trade, and England and France froze all U.S. money earned in their respective countries.

To make matters worse, Disney's latest animated feature, *Pinocchio*, which opened on February 7, 1940, failed to recoup a production budget that had ballooned to $2.6 million. Upcoming projects like *Fantasia* and *Bambi* were already mired in similar cost overruns with little chance of earning a profit, especially given the closure of so many overseas markets. The financial fortunes of the Disney brothers were suddenly in a tailspin.

Roy summoned Walt to his office for a serious talk—never a good sign—and explained that the profits from *Snow White* had been exhausted and the studio was now in debt to the tune of $4.5 million. Roy's only solution was one the brothers had long resisted: an offering of public stock. Walt reluctantly agreed, and on April 2, 1940, Walt Disney Productions made its first public stock offering of 155,000 shares. The move eased the studio's troubles for a time, allowing them to finish their next picture.

But *Fantasia*, which premiered on November 13, 1940, would not provide the financial silver bullet the brothers so desperately needed. The film earned back even less of its $2.28 million budget than *Pinocchio* had. Roy's next solution was much more drastic: a studio-wide 20 percent reduction in costs. This meant a series of hard choices, including the elimination of the popular but expensive *Silly Symphony* shorts. Fortunately, work continued on *Bambi* and two other upcoming, less expensive features: *Dumbo* and the animation/live-action hybrid *The Reluctant Dragon*.

Not all of the studio's troubles were financial. The move to Burbank had caused unrest among longtime staff members used to the camaraderie and freedom of expression the old studio seemingly elicited. And all the creature comforts in the world couldn't mask the fact that direct access to Walt was far more limited here.

"I liked the small place [on Hyperion]. The meetings with Walt we had there were really marvelous," said original Nine Old Men animator Ollie Johnston in a 1973 interview with Walt's biographer Bob Thomas. "He used to get me so enthused. I couldn't wait to get back to my board. He'd get you laughing and all excited

Guests attend the grand opening of *Pinocchio* in the new Studio Theater on April 10, 1940.

Filming of *The Reluctant Dragon* in front of the Studio Theater, 1941.

Animator Bill Justice with a live-action reference fawn during the production of *Bambi* (c. 1940).

about the personality of the guy you were going to work with."

The new studio may have been better organized, but it was also more regimented, partly by sheer necessity: Disney now employed more than a thousand people. The loss of the warm, family atmosphere only emphasized the distance between departments and a burgeoning sense of class distinction between jobs. Less direct communication with Walt also left room for rumors, including a pernicious one that wholesale layoffs were imminent.

Some staffers appreciated Walt's attempts to provide benefits and compensation when waiting for financial prosperity to return. "He became very liberal with his employees. Almost paternalistic," said longtime staffer Dick Huemer. "For instance, he established a savings and loan plan where anyone could get a loan at [a] very small interest, far below the current rate. He instituted a generous bonus system. This had never been done before in the cartoon industry. He gave *paid* vacations, something I had never enjoyed in all my twenty-odd previous years of labor over the light board. He also presented stock to deserving employees."

But others, like Animator Marc Davis, took issue with some of the studio's many perks: "I think an awful lot of frills that [Walt] thought were so wonderful when we first came out to this new building [weren't necessary]," Davis said. "You could order food at any time during the day. You could have a waitress bring in a malted milk. We'd all have weighed three thousand pounds by now if that had continued, or be dead—one or the other. But anyway, there were many, many things of this nature that went by the boards. And I'm sure that [Walt] had to feel that this was a thing against him personally, and I guess in some areas it certainly was." Complaints even began rolling in about the landscaping and the number of waitresses in the commissary.

Recent hires also exploited the mild discontent of the longtime artists, causing a more ominous divide within the ranks. Many of these new folks, who'd been brought in from East Coast studios to work on *Snow White* and subsequent features, did not share a close personal connection to Walt and Roy. They rejected the Disney brothers' paternalism and voiced their desire for an artists' union. After all, Walt Disney Productions already had closed-shop agreements with musicians, cameramen, electricians, costumers, makeup artists, set workers, prop men, and restaurant workers, so why not one for the animators? The Screen Cartoonists Guild agreed.

On May 29, 1941, Walt arrived at work to find a picket line marching outside the Burbank studio's gate. In all, 293 employees, about 40 percent of the staff, according to Disney company records, had opted to strike. In an unfortunate piece of timing, Disney's first live-action film, *The Reluctant Dragon*, featuring a sunny tour of the new studio, opened in theaters on June 20, 1941, right at the height of the strike.

The three-and-a-half-month strike had a profound effect on Walt Disney. In a newspaper interview, he acknowledged feeling "thoroughly disgusted and would gladly quit and try to establish myself in another business if it were not for the loyal guys who believe in me." To combat his frustration, Walt agreed to take part in a goodwill tour of South America, proposed by the Coordinator of Inter-American Affairs (CIAA). The tour was part of a new initiative enlisting Hollywood celebrities to counteract Nazi and fascist influences in South America.

"This South American expedition is a godsend," he said at the time. "I am not so hot for it, but it gives me a chance to get away from this gawd-awful nightmare and bring back some extra work into the plant. I have a case of the D.D.'s—disillusionment and discouragement...."

Never one for downtime, Walt planned to use the trip to make a series of animated films with South American themes. When the company's bank declined to fund the films, the U.S. government agreed to underwrite the expense. Walt handpicked sixteen artists and production staff to accompany him and began extensive research into South American customs, culture, and traditions. On August 17, 1941, "El Grupo" embarked on a three-month tour as part of the United States' Good Neighbor program.

The tour proved a great success both for the CIAA and Walt, who was warmly embraced by the South American public. Following a stop in New York for the *Dumbo* premiere, he arrived home on October 27, 1941, with a wealth of new material that would ultimately become the animated anthology *Saludos Amigos*. Further sweetening his homecoming, Walt learned that the animators strike had finally been settled and, most promisingly, *Dumbo* was a much-needed hit with critics and audiences alike. The movie became so popular, in fact, that *Time* magazine planned to feature the charming but clumsy pachyderm on the cover of an upcoming issue.

The front gate of the Walt Disney Studios, with a Screen Cartoonists Guild picket line (1941).

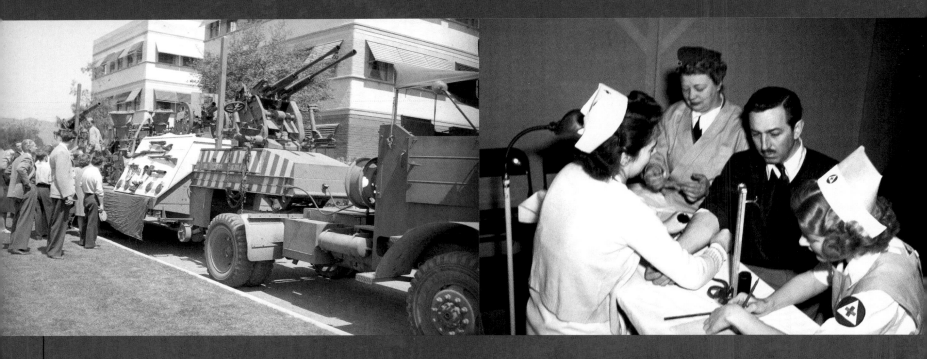

U.S. military antiaircraft guns move onto the lot (1940s).

Walt Disney donates blood during a Red Cross blood drive on the studio lot (1944).

As fate would have it, that issue was slated for publication on December 8, 1941, one day after the Japanese bombing of Pearl Harbor. *Dumbo* would be bumped from *Time*'s cover and the fortunes of the Walt Disney Studios, like those of the entire country, would be changed forever.

Like most Americans, Walt was home that Sunday morning and heard of the attack on the radio. The Burbank studio manager called later that afternoon to inform him that five hundred Army troops were moving onto his new lot. The military planned to use the Disney Studios as an antiaircraft installation to protect the nearby Lockheed Aircraft Company factory, which, as a producer of warplanes, was considered a prime target for possible future attacks.

On Monday, December 8, 1941—less than one year after moving onto the lot—employees arrived at yet another "new" studio. Guards were posted at every gate and the huge, windowless soundstage had been commandeered as a facility to repair military vehicles and antiaircraft guns. Soldiers marched the grounds, mess facilities had sprung up, and camouflage was draped over parking garages and storage sheds, which now doubled as depots for three million rounds of ammunition.

Staffers had little time to adjust to the changes as they were immediately fingerprinted and issued identification badges to wear *at all times!* In the Animation Building, everyone, including Walt and Roy, was forced to share office space and even provide sleeping quarters for soldiers. That evening, Walt received a call from a

Navy official offering him a contract for twenty films on aircraft and warship identification. Disney Studios was now officially a war plant.

"It certainly was novel to come to work in the morning and have to pass armed guards with bayonets drawn," said longtime artist and creative executive John Hench. "And they kept up a strict military procedure. They changed the guard regularly, and they were quartered there. They spent the night in one of our old buildings, which was turned into [a barracks]. It did make a very curious kind of atmosphere, but then of course, the whole world had changed for us. We had a salute going in the morning, and salutes going out. We felt quite comfortable with the military life."

Roy Disney's young son, Roy Edward, remembered "seeing men in uniform everywhere, chain-link fences erected to keep studio employees out of certain areas, and, of course, "walking up and down the halls and seeing artwork everywhere for defense movies of one kind or another.

"I remember going into projection rooms every now and then and being shown—[since] everybody knew I loved airplanes—all the airplane stuff they showed me," Roy E. said. "I do [also] remember there was a commander here, a Navy guy named Thatcher [John S. Thach]. He was a pilot, and he had invented something—a tactic—that they were using against the Japanese, called the Thatcher Weave [Thach Weave]. And it was apparently, as best I recall it, if you could get two guys on the tail of

Mickey Mouse supports home front efforts by appearing on a Civilian Defense poster (1942).

an enemy airplane, the two airplanes learned to do this weave, so that no matter where the prey went, he was in somebody's gunsights. And it was apparently a very, very effective means of air combat. And they got Walt to make an animated version of it to use as a training film, and I remember seeing that one pretty clearly."

The initial Army unit remained at the studio for eight months, until fears of a Japanese attack on the mainland had eased. But they were quickly replaced by other military personnel. Adjusting to working alongside these "outsiders" was difficult for the studio employees; not only did the military have the run of the place, but federal officials and even Lockheed Aircraft's technical production illustrators occupied space on the lot for a time. Story man Joe Grant observed, "The artist, of course, is a revolutionary. He's free. And he wants to do his thing, but in this case, I think they all settled down to the idea that this was war."

Even Walt himself wasn't immune to the challenges. In a 1972 interview with Dave Smith, Carl Nater, the production coordinator for the military educational films, told the story of Walt's unwelcome "houseguest," Raymond Forrest Farwell. Farwell was a captain in the U.S. Naval Reserve and author of *The Rules of the Nautical Road*, which was made into a short film for the Navy. "He was a professor up at Seattle someplace. The University of Washington, I guess," Nater said. "So he came down to the studio to see Walt, and he had just put on his uniform. Yesterday he was a civilian; today he was a captain. Walt was very nice to these fellows, and wanted to make them feel at home."

So when he found out that the captain didn't have a place to stay upon his arrival, Walt kindly offered his office suite until Farwell could find accommodations. "He stayed there over the weekend. Next Monday came, and Tuesday, and Wednesday, he was still there; he wouldn't leave," Nater recalled. "Walt had a little place you could cook there, a little stove or something, so Farwell decided this is great. He was working on a $20 or $30 per diem and here he was getting his rooms free in Walt's office, and he could cook his own food there."

Soon Walt's "guest" was interrupting his day on a regular basis. "To get to that little bedroom, you had to walk through Walt's office," Nater said. "Well, Walt would be having a meeting with

U.S. Naval officers discuss storyboards for an airplane-spotting training film (1942).

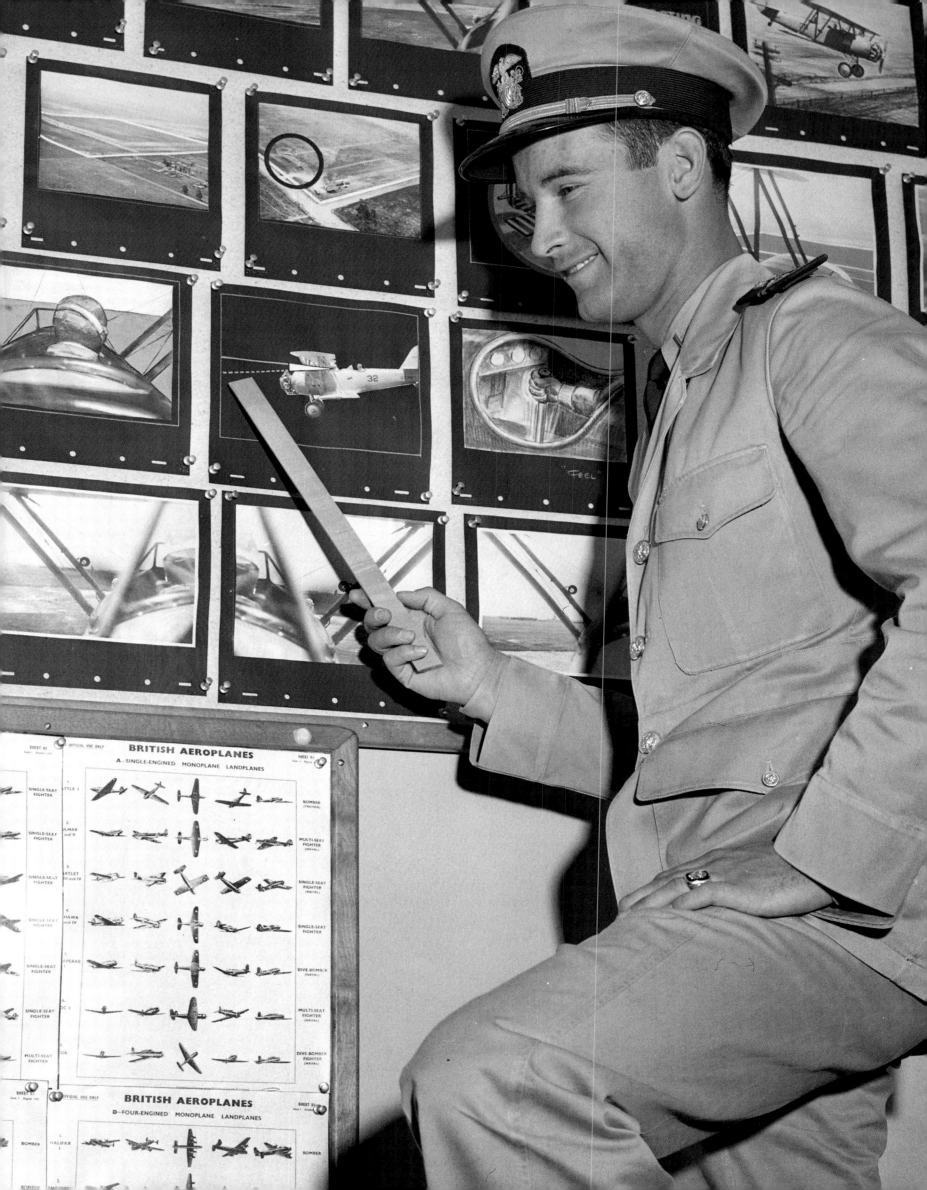

different people in his office and here's Farwell coming in, getting ready for lunch. He'd been to the delicatessen and he'd walk in with his bread and his salami and his little carton of pickles, or something like that, and he'd fix himself a sandwich; then he'd go back in the room to eat it. He literally just took over and Walt didn't know how to get rid of him."

Not all of the studio staffers minded having hundreds of enlisted men living on the lot, however. In a 2004 interview with Didier Ghez, retired Ink and Painter Ruthie Tompson said,

"The girls in Ink and Paint had a lot of fun with the soldiers, and a couple of 'em got married, and so it was very . . . interesting."

Throughout the war, training and propaganda films for every branch of the military, and shorts encouraging the purchase of war bonds and payment of the new "income tax," kept Disney afloat. In fact, the studio produced ten times its usual output of completed film during that span, from an average of thirty thousand to three hundred thousand feet per year!

MILITARY INSIGNIAS

Mickey Mouse and his pals also played an important part in the war effort, as Walt and his team of artists enlisted the Disney characters in many of the military insignias they drafted for Naval vessels, bombing squadrons, training schools, chaplains' corps, women's units, and even Allied units from Britain.

Donald Duck, with his cocky attitude and perennial short fuse, was far and away the most popular choice. Donald appeared in 216 different insignias, including one for prisoners of war in Stalag Luft III, a Nazi prisoner of war camp located near the town of Sagan (now Żagań, Poland).

The official insignia was created at the behest of Captain Robert H. Bishop of the United States Army Air Force, who had been shot down on May 14, 1943, over Kiel, Germany. Captain Bishop sent a postcard to the studio with a rudimentary drawing by fellow POW Flight Lieutenant Brian Evans of a very frustrated Donald Duck drumming his fingers behind bars. The sketch had become the camp's unofficial insignia and Lieutenant Evans was called upon to draw it often to boost morale.

Walt wrote back offering to make up the insignia in cloth and send four dozen to the prisoners. "We have made hundreds of insignias for Allied groups the world over," Walt wrote, "but this is the first request we have had from any of our American boys in prison camps."

Due to the long waiting list for fabric insignias, the studio was not able to provide the cloth patches as planned, but the professionally drawn image was sent to Captain Bishop. The rest of the Stalag Luft III story is a pretty famous one—at least to movie fans. It's the real-life location and inspiration for the 1963 film *The Great Escape*.

Another set of well-known insignias featured some rather adorable pests created by Flight Lieutenant Roald Dahl of the British Royal Air Force. Dahl, the soon-to-be famous writer of children's books like *Charlie and the Chocolate Factory*, *James and the Giant Peach*, and *Matilda*, wrote a story called "Gremlin Lore," which was about mythical imps that cause air disasters for pilots.

Walt was intrigued by the idea and the two began collaborating on an animated feature film called *The Gremlins*. Dahl wrote the story and Disney studio artists illustrated it, creating a new world of Gremlins, Spandules, Widgets, and female Fifinellas.

Unfortunately, the film never made it past the story stage, but Dahl's characters were published in a children's book and the Gremlin sketches would travel the world as part of numerous military insignias.

"Disney in those days—we were kind of a one-trick pony; we had a feature every year or every other year and some short subjects. And that's who we were. That was it," remembered Roy E. "And Walt always spent more than Dad [Roy O. Disney] could raise, and there was sort of an eternal Ponzi scheme, in a sense, going on: that this one made enough to pay off that debt so that we could raise the debt by some further amount on the next one.

"In the wartime, of course, they mostly were making these films for the government for flat fees," Roy E. added, "and I remember clearly my dad saying [to Walt], 'I don't care how much they give you, you'll still spend more than they give you.' And, you know, Walt, he couldn't help himself. You gotta make it better. You can't just stop now after the money's spent. So an awful lot of that was on our nickel, and that was tough because just keeping the paychecks coming was tough."

Grant recalled that, even with the war films, Walt insisted on Disney-level quality. "We got cost plus 10 percent or something like that, which he overran in every case, so I think that was Walt's greatest contribution as far as the war effort was concerned," he said.

Both Disney brothers faced enormous pressure: Walt to keep the production pipeline moving, and Roy to keep the studio in business. Roy E. said of his father, "I used to kid that I could tell when he'd had a bad day by the way he drove into the driveway, and the way he slammed the door of his car, and I'd sort of duck around the corner. He really, in truth, didn't bring it home too much. He and mother, I think, discussed it more than certainly he would have in front of a kid, but it was hard times for everybody. We had ration stamps, and we had missing servicemen stars in windows, and we had rationed meat and rationed butter, and we were growing vegetables in the victory garden, and you never forgot it, so it was always there."

As part of the war effort, Walt also handpicked some of his studio artists to create illustrations for home front groups like the United Service Organizations (USO) and Community Chest and insignia designs for military units. All the work was provided free of charge and became so popular among the service units that by 1947, more than 1,200 unique designs had been developed. When asked how he could supply that much unpaid work, Walt replied, "I had to do it. Those kids grew up on Mickey Mouse. I owed it to 'em."

In April 1942, Walt turned his focus to a new war-related project. Former Russian pilot Major Alexander P. de Seversky had recently published a treatise on how to end the war, *Victory Through Air Power*. The best-selling book was met with skepticism by critics, but Walt was an instant believer. He reached out to Major de Seversky and by July had a deal in place to adapt the book for the screen.

Animator Roy Williams looks on as studio artist Hank Porter draws a new military insignia (1941).

Happy the Dwarf on a military insignia for the USS *Jason* (ARJ-1), Los Angeles Shipbuilding & Dry Dock Corp., San Pedro, California.

An RKO actress poses for the centaurette insignia created for the Women's Civil Air Force of Greater St. Louis, Pine Lawn, Missouri (1942).

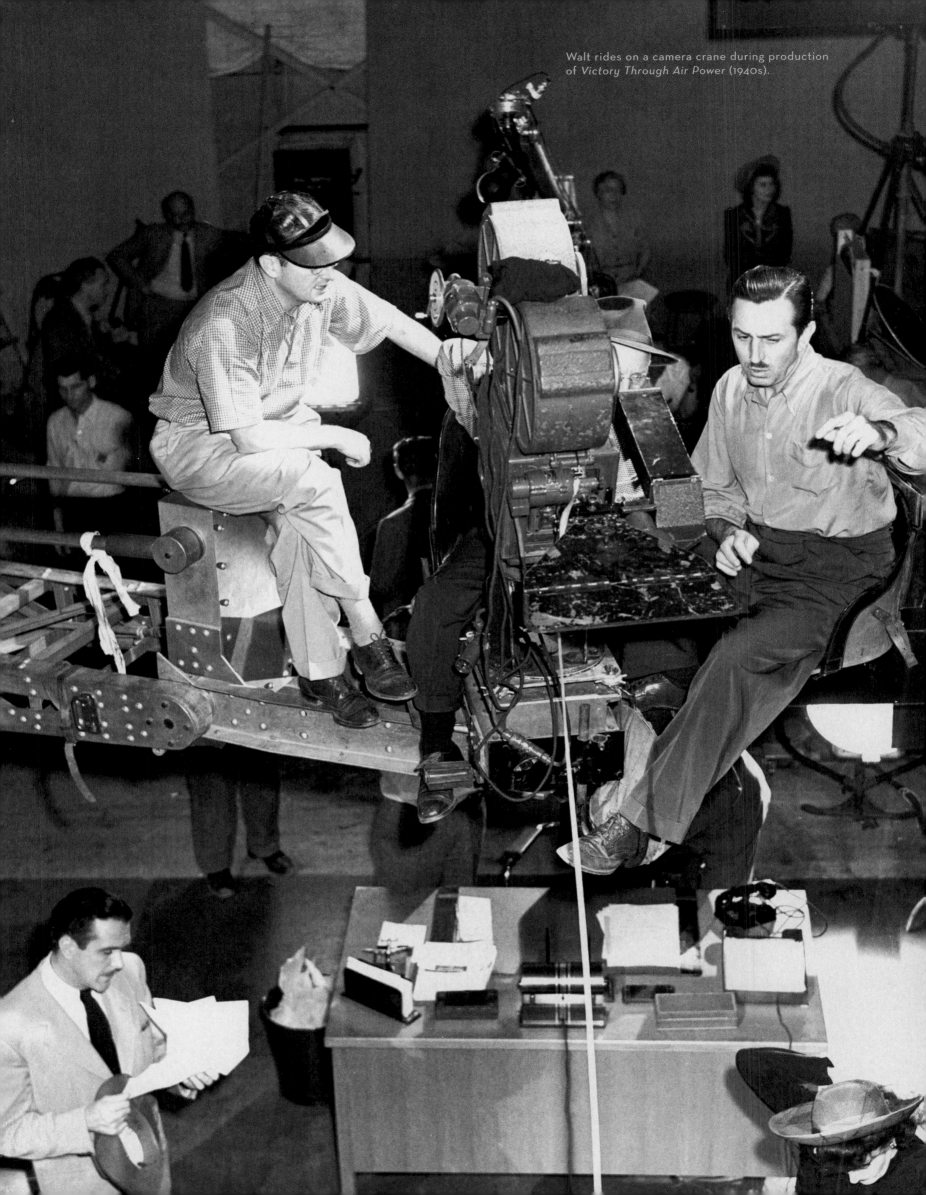

Walt rides on a camera crane during production of *Victory Through Air Power* (1940s).

Walt Disney supervises production of *Victory Through Air Power* (1940s).

Military insignia created for U.S. Navy Scouting Squadron No. 11, U.S.N. C/O P.M., San Francisco (1943).

"It helped the studio out," said animator John Hench. "We were kind of low on work. We hadn't started a picture, and I guess it kind of impressed Walt because he made that picture *Victory Through Air Power*. He went ahead and finished that on the fringe of the work we had done. He was impressed by these people."

The movie began production in early October 1942, shooting at night to avoid the constant roar of jet engines from the nearby Lockheed plant. The finished project, released in 1943, was a masterful blend of live action and animation that served as a tutorial on the ways long-range airpower could be used to crush Japan and the other Axis powers.

Roy E. reminisced, "We went [to the movie] as a family—Mother and Dad and me, and Walt and Lilly and Diane—all [of us] went to New York for the premiere of *Victory Through Air Power*. And we all went and we stayed in some hotel near where the theater was in [the city]; and of course that was long before there was air-conditioning, and it was summer and all the windows were open—wide-open windows on the fortieth floor of a hotel with little kids in the room!

"Diane and I got together, and there was a big pad of hotel stationery," Roy E. recounted further, "and we got crayons out and we started writing 'Go See *Victory Through Air Power*' at the such-and-such theater; 'Opens Today,' or something like that. And we formed these into paper gliders and threw them out the window. And we thought this was really a brilliant publicity campaign. Airplanes were coming out

of the sky advertising a movie about airpower. I have always wondered if anyone picked one of those things up."

The Disney family's early attempt at guerrilla marketing would fall short, however, as *Victory Through Air Power* lost nearly half a million dollars at the box office. But there was no denying the film's impact on public support for the war at a time when the Allies were attempting to turn the tide. Prominent radio broadcaster Fulton Lewis Jr. raved, "This is a powerful motion picture, which everyone interested in victory must see!" while *Redbook* heralded it as "a breathless story developed with imaginative sweep and power." Famed Hollywood gossip columnist Hedda Hopper called the movie "one of the most stupendous things ever put on the screen!"

Winston Churchill, prime minister of Great Britain, was also quite taken with *Victory Through Air Power*, as was President Franklin Roosevelt, who had a copy flown in by fighter jet and showed it to his Joint Chiefs of Staff. This screening also played an important part in the decision by Allied military strategists to provide the 1944 D-Day invasion forces hitting the French coast around Normandy with sufficient air support.

"It was a stupid thing to do as a business venture," Walt would say with hindsight. "[But] it was just something that I believed in, and for no other reason than that, I did it."

Disney Studios was not completely focused on

making films for the government and military during World War II. A year before *Victory Through Air Power* came out, the studio released two pictures in 1942. One, the long-gestating *Bambi* premiered on August 8 to lukewarm box office receipts and mixed reviews. It would be the last completely animated feature film the studio released for eight years. The second, was a feature film comprised of Walt's South American shorts. The shorts, featuring Donald Duck and his Brazilian parrot friend José Carioca, were cobbled together with live-action production footage ("home movies") taken by Walt during the CIAA trip, and a few humorous staged scenes shot at the studio for release as *Saludos Amigos* (or *Hello, Friends*). This film, the first in a series of Disney "Package Films," premiered in Brazil on August 24.

Work soon began on a sequel, *The Three Caballeros*, starring the same lovable "birds of a feather," Donald and José, along with a gun-toting Mexican charro rooster named Panchito. The live-action portions of this film were partially shot on what would become the Walt Disney Studios back lot, an undeveloped tract of land that doubled as Mexico's sunny Acapulco beach filled with huge umbrellas and Latin beauties in swimsuits. *The Three Caballeros* premiered in Mexico City on December 21, 1944, and in New York on February 3, 1945, but would only serve to exacerbate the studio's prolonged box office slump.

But good news was, finally, on the horizon. On September 2, 1945, Japan surrendered to the Allies, formally ending World War II. Walt wanted to immediately resume work on his postponed animated features, but Roy, over the course of several heated arguments, convinced him otherwise.

"The end of the war has given us the chance to go ahead with plans which until now we could only think about. It has also confronted us with a number of problems," Walt wrote in the 1945 Walt Disney Productions Annual Report for employees.

With the studio's financial resources depleted, the Disney brothers opted to focus on producing more package films of cartoon shorts. The first, *Make Mine Music*, mimicked the style of *Fantasia* using contemporary music; *Fun and*

The studio's Buena Vista parking lot stands in for Mexico's "Acapulco Beach" in *The Three Caballeros* (c. 1944).

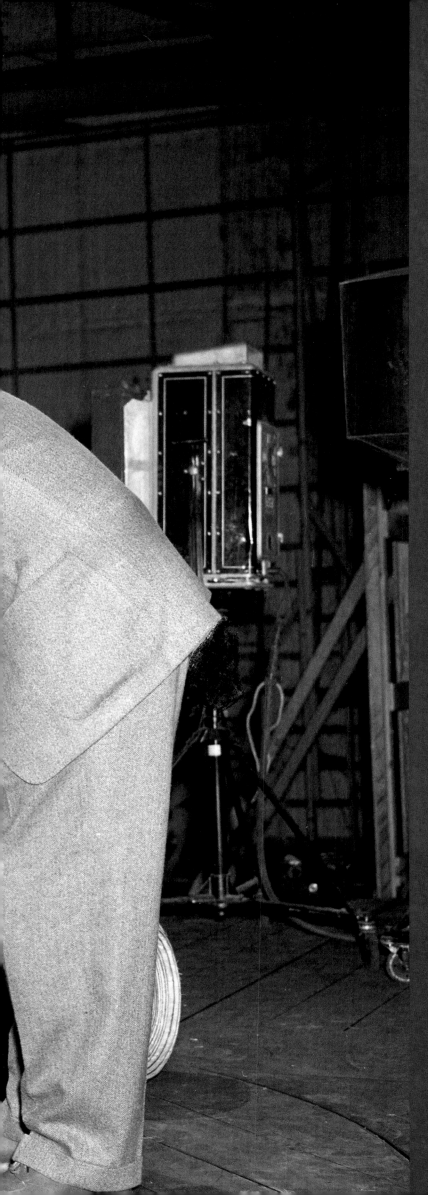

Fancy Free, *Melody Time*, and *The Adventures of Ichabod and Mr. Toad* soon followed over the next few years.

"We did those anthology films—*Make Mine Music* and *Melody Time*—and of course, *Saludos Amigos* and *The Three Caballeros* were made toward the end of the war, and none of them really did a lot of business," Roy E. said, noting that the studio's distributor, RKO, quickly grew tired of these anthologies.

Walt also continued exploring the comparatively cheap world of live-action filmmaking with two new hybrid live-action/animation features after World War II ended: *Song of the South* and *So Dear to My Heart*. Both movies, shot on location away from the studio, signaled a growing focus on live-action films.

Reflecting on the war years, with the military occupation of the studio and its aftermath, Roy E. said, "I think probably in the end, it was kind of a bitter memory because we had to stop doing what we were best at and do things that had to be done. And I'm sure everybody had as much fun as you could have doing them, but nonetheless, not really fun. And a lot of the personalities that were a part of the early days had gone off and served their country for some time, and so there was kind of a homecoming when they came back, and that was good."

The studio's fortunes, indeed its future, remained very much in doubt, however, as Walt and his artists turned their attention to their first fully animated feature in nearly a decade, a story that would soon become synonymous with remarkable transformations: *Cinderella*.

Walt and organist Ethel Smith consult during production of the "Blame It on the Samba" sequence of *Melody Time* (1945).

WALT'S CINDERELLA STORY

Jeffrey Stone and Helene Stanley perform
live-action reference for *Cinderella* (1948).

Few in the Walt Disney Studios family likely shed tears as the 1940s drew to a close. A decade that began with so much promise had delivered mostly hardships: a World War, a labor strike, and a mounting series of inventive but financially disappointing movies. But with a new decade came new hope as Disney Studios prepared to debut its first animated feature film in eight years.

Cinderella would either be Disney's *magnum opus* or its swan song. No one saw that more clearly than Walt himself. Already in debt to the tune of $4 million, he and Roy poured all the studio's remaining resources into the project. Walt also broke from tradition by assigning all of his "Nine Old Men"—the group of legendary animators who served as the creative backbone of Disney animation—to the project. Typically, they divided their talents over several different productions. As he had in the early days, Walt oversaw every aspect of the project.

His biggest challenge, as with *Snow White and the Seven Dwarfs*, was finding a way to make a very old story feel new. Every child already knew by heart the story of the beautiful young Cinderella, forced into servitude at the hands of an abusive stepmother and cruel stepsisters. So Walt and his team created vibrant supporting characters, enchanting environments, and memorable songs that added new dimensions to the classic fairy tale. Characters like Cinderella's bird and mice friends, particularly Jaq and Gus, and the true-blue hound dog, Bruno, account

for much of the humor and heart of the story as they combat the sinister antics of another Disney fabrication, Stepmother's villainous cat, Lucifer.

Ilene Woods, the voice of Cinderella, recalled one particularly memorable moment during production: "We had finished recording 'Sing, Sweet Nightingale' and Walt came in at the end of the day. He'd always listen to our recordings with his head down, resting in his hands. This particular time he looked up at me and asked, 'Ilene, can you sing harmony with yourself? I envision Cinderella scrubbing the floor and a soap bubble rise, and I hear a second-part harmony begin. Then I see another soap bubble rise and hear a third-part harmony kick in and so on and so on until we've got about an eight-part harmony going.'

"So, he had me sing the song and then record the second-part harmony and so on," Ilene said. "They mixed all the parts together, and it was such a beautiful animation sequence because each time a bubble would rise, so would another voice and it blended so well because it was all the same voice. When I heard the finished product, Walt said, 'How about that? All of these years I've been paying three salaries for the Andrews Sisters [who performed in both *Melody Time* and *Make Mine Music*], when I could have paid only one for you!'"

The effect was intoxicating, a quintessential Disney moment whose charm is rivaled only by musical sequences like "Bibbidi-Bobbidi-Boo"

Helene Stanley is coached by Director Wilfred Jackson for the live-action reference of *Cinderella* (1948).

Jeffrey Stone and Helene Stanley perform live-action reference for *Cinderella* (1948).

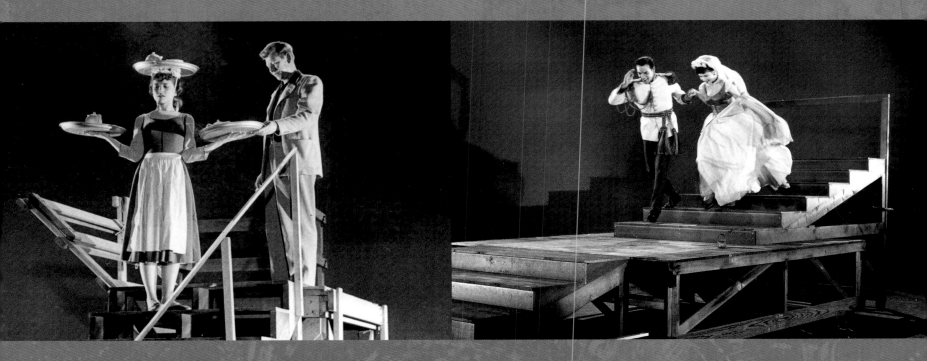

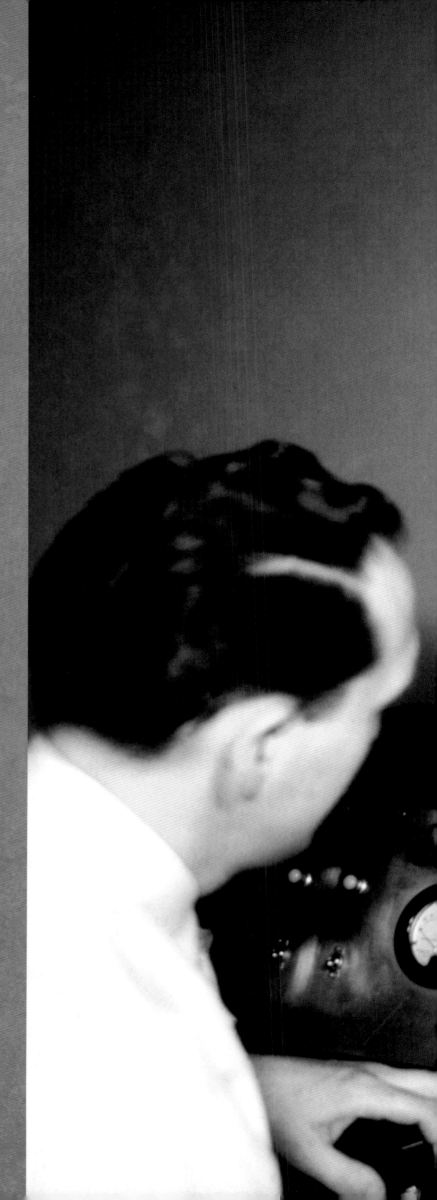

and "A Dream Is a Wish Your Heart Makes" within the movie.

The studio buzzed with nervous excitement as the film's February release date approached. This was, after all, the biggest risk of Walt's career: failure would doom the animated film program and likely close the Burbank dream factory. But that doomsday scenario never materialized: *Cinderella* was both an astounding success and a self-fulfilling prophecy for Disney. Audiences swarmed to theaters, bringing in more than $4 million in domestic box office receipts alone. Critics were equally enchanted, bestowing Walt an Academy Award nomination for the song "Bibbidi-Bobbidi-Boo."

Cinderella was heralded as a rebirth for both Disney animation and the studio itself, ushering in an era where Walt reigned over his empire like a modern-day Midas. He immediately reinstituted his production pipeline, developing a string of animation masterpieces with rare missteps. Ironically, one of those missteps was Disney's next animated film.

That film, *Alice in Wonderland*, premiered in the summer of 1951. While clever and visually impressive, the movie lacked the warmth and empathy audiences expected from the makers of *Snow White* and *Dumbo*. Animator Ward Kimball dismissed the film as "a loudmouthed vaudeville show," the result of the scattershot way it had been produced.

Alice featured five different directors overseeing different segments of the movie. Each director, according to Kimball, tried to "make his sequences the biggest and craziest in the show," resulting in a chaotic "self-canceling effect on the final product." Ironically, Kimball pointed out, all of the "mad" sequences—from the tea party to the Caterpillar to Tweedledee and Tweedledum—were eclipsed by his Cheshire Cat character "because compared to the constant, all-out, wild gyrations of the other characters, [the Cheshire Cat] played it real cool. His quiet, underplayed subtleties consequently stole the show."

Indeed, the Cheshire Cat, with his exasperatingly funny, yet understated antics, remains one of the film's most memorable figures. Critics widely panned the movie upon its release,

Ilene Woods records the voice of *Cinderella* (1949).

Live-action reference of Kathryn Beaumont as Alice for *Alice in Wonderland* (1950).

Matching cel frame of Alice drifting in the bottle (1951).

and the initial public response was tepid, though public opinion has softened over time; *Alice in Wonderland* is now considered a bona fide Disney classic.

The next animated feature, *Peter Pan*, fulfilled a dream Walt had harbored since the earliest days of his studio: "I was unwilling to start until I could do full justice to the well-loved story. Animation techniques were constantly improving, but they still fell short of what I felt was needed to tell the story of *Peter Pan* as I saw it. When we finally sat down to go to work, we

faced a real challenge. *Peter Pan* is a work of sheer magic, and you do not create magic to order."

By this point Disney felt he could meet that challenge. Still, "We had to somehow re-create the essence of make-believe and do it in such a way that millions of people who had known and loved [Sir James M.] Barrie's play since it was first performed in 1904 would recognize it and approve of what we had done," Walt noted.

Walt let Barrie's own words ("Nothing of importance ever happens to us after we reach the

Live-action reference of the "Mad Tea Party" scene with actors Ed Wynn, Kathryn Beaumont, and studio animators (1949).

Walt Disney and Bobby Driscoll during live-action reference filming for *Peter Pan* (in 1951).

Margaret Kerry provides live-action reference for Tinker Bell in *Peter Pan* (in 1951).

age of twelve" and "Oh, that we might be boys and girls all our lives") be his guide. No adult experience, he realized, can ever surpass the newness, whimsy, and wonder of childhood. As such, his adaptation was filled with imaginative additions and exciting new twists on the classic tale. For the first time, a boy portrayed Peter and the Darling children's trustworthy dog, Nana, would be an actual canine instead of a human actor. Audiences also got to see—instead of imagine—the Crocodile and Tinker Bell, a real pixie rather than a speck of light.

Creating Tinker Bell was a particular challenge for Animator Marc Davis, who literally started from scratch (paper). Contrary to popular myth, the fairy wasn't modeled on the persona and physique of Marilyn Monroe, who had yet to ascend to stardom during *Peter Pan*'s production. Tink's design was actually based on a live-action model, Margaret Kerry, who shot her film footage at the studio on Stage One.

"Cartoonists, just like artists, must have living models to draw from," Director Hamilton Luske explained to a UPI reporter. "Otherwise, they'd

Roland Dupree provides live-action reference for *Peter Pan* (1951).

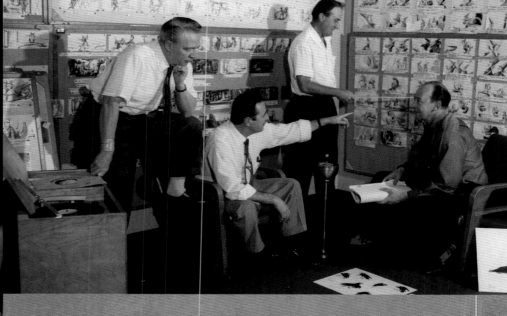

Story session during the production of *Sleeping Beauty*. Left to right: Eric Larson, Joe Rinaldi, Don DaGradi, and Marc Davis (in 1957).

be drawing what they think certain characters would do in a situation, not what they really would do. We could, of course, have the live models act out a scene on a stage. But then the animators would have to trust their memories when they go back to their drawing boards. A film is easier, as it can be run over and over for the artists. And they can correct any mistakes in a scene before the drawing is made."

Peter Pan delivered on Walt's goal to "re-create a children's world, but a children's world in which adults could find a place. Its blend of warm humor and pacing, dynamic characters, and catchy songs was a critical and commercial success and the top-grossing film of 1953, earning approximately $7 million against a $4 million production budget. Through theatrical reissues and home entertainment releases, the movie remains one of Disney's most successful animated titles.

Following *Peter Pan* and *Lady and the Tramp*, Disney's next picture, *Sleeping Beauty*, would undergo a forced slumber of its own before its eventual release. Development on the project began shortly after *Cinderella's* sensationally successful run but was postponed in 1954 so studio resources could be diverted to the construction of Disneyland. Finally released in 1959, the film was arguably Walt's most lavish production to date—a moving tapestry of medieval, gothic beauty that proved animation was indeed a form of art.

Studio cameramen shoot a sequence for *Sleeping Beauty* on one of the studio animation cameras (in 1957).

Live-action reference for Cruella De Vil in *One Hundred and One Dalmatians* (1958).

A work of such sophistication and style came at a steep price, however. *Sleeping Beauty* was, at $6 million, the most expensive animated film ever made, and its respectable box office failed to recoup the investment. But Walt had finally learned his lesson. The movie marked the end of the extravagant era in Disney animation as the studio turned its focus to less expensive artistic styles without sacrificing the quality and innovation fans had come to expect. In fact, 1961's *One Hundred and One Dalmatians*, with its simplified but stylized approach and rough-lined animation technique, won both critical and public acclaim at a price tag $2 million less than its predecessor.

The Jungle Book was sadly the last animated feature to be overseen by Walt. In some ways, the project felt cursed from the start. Walt entrusted veteran story man Bill Peet, who was largely responsible for *One Hundred and One Dalmatians* and 1963's *The Sword in the Stone*, to develop the script. But Peet's dark, brooding take, similar in tone to Rudyard Kipling's original novel, failed to impress the boss. An ensuing battle of wills—and harsh words—led to Peet's departure from Disney.

Walt then brought together his creative team, including songwriting brothers Richard and Robert Sherman, and asked how many of them had read the original Kipling book. The room, according to composer Richard Sherman, "was silent. 'Good, I don't want you to read the book,' Walt said. 'Now here's the story.'" And much as he had with *Snow White* so many years before, he began to perform *his* version of *The Jungle Book*. "Walt acted out the movements of Baloo the Bear in the hall after a meeting. He invented this little step I had Baloo do, which was the key to his personality," Animator Ollie Johnston recalled.

While shepherding the new movie through development with his usual verve, Walt was also—quietly—battling illness. Some on the team knew of his frequent visits to the hospital across the street, but they assumed it was related to back pain from his polo injury sustained years earlier. The truth was far graver: lung cancer.

On December 15, 1966, news began to circulate throughout the studio that Walt had died. He was only sixty-five years old. Some sat at their desks in utter silence and disbelief while others burst into helpless tears. Quite a few staffers simply gathered their belongings and headed home. "Walt was like a father figure to everybody," said story man and Animator Burny Mattinson. "You just don't think father is ever going to get sick or certainly going to die."

But, as had always been the case, Walt had a plan in place. During the late stages of his illness, he summoned Woolie Reitherman, one of his trusted Nine Old Men, to the hospital for an important conversation. He wanted Reitherman to take control of the animated features department and ensure Disney's upcoming projects moved forward. Under Reitherman's leadership, the team completed *The Jungle Book*, careful at every stage to see Walt's vision for the film was realized.

The final product, which premiered in 1967, bore little resemblance to the bleak Kipling book on which it was based. "It's possibly the most bright and breezy, freewheeling, happy-go-lucky, upbeat of all [of] Disney's movies," noted Disney historian Brian Sibley. While certainly not the flashiest or grandest of the studio's artistic achievements, *The Jungle Book* was an extraordinary showcase of the best Disney characters, storytelling, and music.

The film was also, to no one's surprise, a phenomenal success, second only to *The Graduate* in box office receipts that year with $13 million. Critics praised it, with the *New York Times* calling the picture "a perfect dandy cartoon feature...grand fun for all ages"; *Life* magazine's Richard Schickel was just as effusive, saying it was "the best thing of its kind since *Dumbo*."

More importantly, the film served as a source of pride for the men and women at Walt Disney Studios, a fitting tribute to their beloved boss. As Hazel George, the studio lot's nurse, and a confidant of Walt's, told Ollie Johnston following a staff screening. "Walt wasn't a man, he was a force of nature. And that last scene where Baloo and Bagheera dance off into the sunset, you know, that's just the way Walt went off. He went off into the sunset. Just like that, and there, he's gone."

Jazz great Louis Prima and his band record "I Wanna Be Like You" for *The Jungle Book* on Stage A (c. 1965).

OF MIDAS AND MOVIES

Dick Van Dyke and Julie Andrews rehearse the
"Jolly Holiday" sequence of *Mary Poppins* (c. 1963).

In the spring of 1954, Walt found himself in all-too-familiar territory as he prepared to shoot another ambitious, technically daunting film based on a literary masterpiece. The project, a live-action adaptation of Jules Verne's *20,000 Leagues Under the Sea*, would take a full year to complete and cost more than double its planned budget on its way to becoming the most expensive movie ever made (at the time). In other words, it was just the sort of nightmare Walt and Roy had hoped to avoid when they began exploring the world of completely live-action.

Walt and Roy's live-action initiative began during the dark days of the late 1940s, when the lingering effects of World War II and the company's slate of expensive and underperforming animated films had threatened to close Disney's gates forever. Live-action films, with their abbreviated production timeline and comparatively low cost, provided an avenue to desperately needed revenue.

Their two early forays into this genre, *Song of the South* and *So Dear to My Heart*, retained some of the animation for which Walt was so well known. In 1950, the studio released its first purely live-action feature, *Treasure Island*. The movie, starring Disney favorite Bobby Driscoll, received wide acclaim, and three more action-adventure pictures would follow: *The Story of Robin Hood and His Merrie Men*; *The Sword and the Rose*; and *Rob Roy, the Highland Rogue*. All four films were shot in England, where Disney had funds languishing due to strict postwar export regulations.

The studio had also experienced unexpected success with its newly minted *True-Life Adventure* featurettes, which showcased eye-popping wonders of nature through the masterful lens of cinematographers Alfred and Elma Milotte. The Milottes captured the animal kingdom at its most stunning, much to the utter delight of theater audiences. The Academy of Motion Picture Arts and Sciences also took note, awarding Disney five Oscars for the featurettes, starting with 1948's *Seal Island*.

Given their enormous popularity, Disney made plans in 1953 to release a full-length *True-Life Adventure* title, *The Living Desert*. But much as they had initially with *Seal Island*, longtime distributor RKO lacked Walt's enthusiasm for the project and refused to release it. The decision would signal the end of the relationship. Walt and Roy broke with RKO and placed their fortunes—and profits—in their own hands by founding the Buena Vista Distribution Company, named for the street on which Walt Disney Studios was located.

Their first release was, of course, *The Living Desert*, which tallied an impressive $5 million in box office receipts from an investment of $500,000 in production costs. The film was a critical and audience favorite as well, earning yet another Oscar for Best Documentary Feature and proving that Walt Disney's golden

Walt presents his visitor with a glimpse at the studio's newest fantastical creation, the giant squid from *20,000 Leagues Under the Sea* (in 1954).

Kirk Douglas gets a smooch from costar Esmeralda during production of *20,000 Leagues Under the Sea* (c. 1953).

James Mason prepares for an underwater sequence in *20,000 Leagues Under the Sea* (c. 1953).

touch was not limited to the world of animation.

And then came *20,000 Leagues Under the Sea*. Walt had long admired Jules Verne's novel, but given the logistical challenges of bringing the story to the screen, he always envisioned it as an animated feature. Disney artist Harper Goff, another ardent fan of the book, would convince him otherwise. In a classic moment of "while the cat's away . . . ," Goff developed a series of story sketches while Walt was traveling for business. He made his pitch upon Disney's return . . . and Walt was immediately sold!

Disney's vision for *20,000 Leagues* was characteristically extravagant, with an estimated budget of $2.7 million that surpassed *Gone with the Wind*. The film would require an aggressive underwater shooting schedule, large-scale yet intricate sets, and top-shelf special effects, including a functional giant squid. Walt was, as to be expected, undaunted by these challenges. "He was somebody who had absolute confidence in what he was doing," said John Hench.

Within Hollywood circles, this confidence was perceived to be more like hubris. Walt and his team were seen as little more than cartoon producers who lacked the experience necessary for a live-action film of such magnitude. Much as they had decades earlier with *Snow White*, many predicted the death knell when news of Disney's latest project hit the trade papers. But those within the studio gates did not share this grim assessment; Walt had always been, as matte artist Peter Ellenshaw noted, "a great gambler."

He was also an unconventional thinker, as he proved with his choice of director of the film— Richard Fleischer. Fleischer's father, Max, had created the popular *Out of the Inkwell* animated comedies, which inspired Disney's early Alice comedies. Disney's rise to prominence, ultimately, had turned the two men into rivals. "So it was a great surprise to me when Walt offered me the job," said Richard Fleischer. He told Walt, "I would love to do this more than anything in the world. This is exactly what I've been looking for, hoping for. But since we have a situation with my father, I wouldn't want him to feel that I was somehow being disloyal to him by working for you."

Fleischer phoned his father who was in New York to explain the situation, and Max urged him to take the job: "'You must by all means, you must take that job,'" Richard recalled his father saying. "'But tell Walt something for me. Give him a message. You tell Walt he's got great taste in directors.'"

With his production team in place, Walt was now ready to begin work on *20,000 Leagues Under the Sea*, even if his studio wasn't. A $300,000 soundstage—Stage Three—with a water tank with depths ranging from three- to eighteen-feet-deep, was constructed to accommodate the story's many underwater and seafaring sequences, including the climactic battle with a giant squid.

The film's iconic submarine, the *Nautilus*, also needed to be built. Goff "whittled out a model" for Walt combining futuristic piston-driven mechanisms with Victorian-era adornments, so the ship's eccentric commander, Captain

Nemo, could be surrounded by rich, tasteful furnishings while engaging in his mad quest for revenge. "Nothing looks more attractive than a combination of rough iron and elegant luxury," Goff said. Remarkably, his original "whittled" model was identical to the final version, with one alteration from the boss himself. Befitting the atomic age in which they lived, Walt suggested the *Nautilus* run on nuclear energy rather than electricity as in Verne's novel. A few years later, the U.S. Navy would christen its first nuclear sub, the *Nautilus*, in a nod to the film.

The exhaustive design work would continue with the submarine's practical sets, including a 150-foot replica of the deck to be shot on Stage Three, another full-scale replica for exterior shots, and elaborate interiors, as well as large-scale "miniatures" for effects shots. "The set was designed so that you could see the entire set in almost every shot—the walls and the floor and the ceiling. We wanted that to give us a feeling of claustrophobia, to feel as if you are enclosed in that submarine," Fleischer, the director, said.

Not all of the set work was quite so elaborate:

Production of *20,000 Leagues Under the Sea* in the water tank of Stage Three (c. 1953).

The use of forced perspective required a huge set for King Brian's Hall in *Darby O'Gill and the Little People* (c. 1958).

John Hench recalled using color wheels behind clear plastic salad bowls from the local dime store for the *Nautilus*'s atomic furnace. And what filled in as Captain Nemo's iconic pipe organ? A defunct electric theater organ set designer Emile Kuri purchased for $50 through an advertisement someone had posted at a locale in the surrounding San Fernando Valley. Kuri simply cast the pipes in plaster and covered them in gold leaf. The organ (minus the film's pipes) is still in use today, as the centerpiece of the *Haunted Mansion*'s ballroom at Disneyland.

But such financial shortcuts were rare and often undone by other expenditures, including the on-screen talent. A movie of this size needed marquee names—James Mason, Kirk Douglas, Peter Lorre, and Paul Lukas—and such stars didn't come cheaply; nor did the experimental underwater diving gear and camera equipment required for filming several scenes. Arguably, the costliest aspect of the project would become known without affection as "the sunset squid fight," which Fleischer called "absolute total disaster in every sense of the word."

No one could have predicted the exorbitant amount of money, time, and sheer aggravation screenwriter Earl Felton's simple description would cause: "THE NAUTILUS breaks the surface in the red after-glow of sunset, the ugly body of the squid silhouetted against the horizon, its long tentacles writhing."

The deep red sky, intended to set a tense, dramatic tone, instead made everything look ridiculous. And the movie's incredibly expensive, "fully functioning" seventy-foot-tall giant squid was worthless, "a great big blob of something," according to Fleischer. The tentacles were operated from above by puppeteers pulling heavy cables that were painfully visible at every angle against the crimson sky.

"It was just impossible," Fleischer said. "So, I'm trying to shoot this thing, and I'm sick to my stomach looking at it because I know it's not working."

The horrific footage was nonetheless shown to Walt who was underwhelmed to say the least. "'I just saw your dailies. I've been watching what you're doing here. You're making a Keystone Kops comedy movie. This is terrible,'" Fleischer recalled Walt saying. The director bemoaned his shooting struggles with the giant squid and Walt decided to seek out his "geniuses at Disneyland."

But it was ultimately Felton, the unwitting cause of the problem, who came up with a solution. He told Fleischer, "This should be a sequence that takes place at night in a violent storm with lightning and thunder and wind, tremendous wind, waves smashing everything, so it becomes not just a fight against the squid, but a fight against nature as well. You'll only see the

squid really in flashes of lightning and you won't see any flaws that it may have."

But Felton's idea came at a price, another $250,000 that was added to an already bloated budget. A more functional and realistic squid was built—a two-ton, fully operational monstrosity that used vacuum hoses to move its tentacles and required a crew of twenty-eight men to operate. The *Nautilus* also needed to be reengineered so it would tilt during the fight with the squid; and thirty costly wind machines, wave makers, water cannons, and huge dunk tanks were brought in to help enhance the fight scene. The wind machines, really just old airplane engines with caged propellers, did a masterful job in creating the climactic storm. "They'd just crank them at full throttle, pouring fire hoses of water into the wind stream so the rain was coming sideways," Walt's nephew, Roy E. Disney, who was working at the studio at this time, recalled.

By all accounts, it was a spectacle beyond compare. Water a foot deep flowed out of the soundstage during the shoot, and three crew members later fell ill with pneumonia, but the hurricane-force storm and the new squid made for an extraordinarily convincing fight scene. The skyrocketing costs of the project forced Walt and Roy to seek out financiers, who were persuaded to supply another $1.5 million after seeing the breathtaking footage.

Ultimately, the movie would take two years to complete and cost an unthinkable-at-the-time $9 million when the price of its massive advertising campaign was factored in. But Walt's arguably biggest gamble to date would pay off: *20,000 Leagues Under the Sea* was a worldwide hit, both critically and commercially. The film won two Oscars and cemented Walt's reputation as a serious and successful filmmaker.

More live-action hits followed, including the tear-jerking adventure *Old Yeller*, starring *Mickey Mouse Club* favorites Tommy Kirk and Kevin Corcoran. The studio's first live-action comedy, *The Shaggy Dog*, with Fred MacMurray in the first of many Disney roles, followed later in the decade. But it was a film about "little people" that proved to be Disney's next big challenge.

Darby O'Gill and the Little People, released in 1959, carried Walt back to his Irish roots, as he explored the lore and legend of the wily King Brian and his mischievous leprechauns. The film was directed by Robert Stevenson, who *Variety* would later call "the most commercially successful director in the history of films."

The grand scope of *Darby O'Gill* would once again require the construction of a large new soundstage on the lot and extensive special effects, including several elaborate sequences in the leprechaun cave. Disney was at the time the only Hollywood studio with its own in-

Tommy Kirk transforms into The Shaggy Dog through the magic of the studio Makeup Department (c. 1958).

house effects department, a necessary luxury given Walt's fondness for stories and locations that were impossible to re-create by traditional means. Fortunately, effects wizards like Peter Ellenshaw possessed the skills and creativity required to bring to life whatever wild idea the boss might conceive.

Ellenshaw, who worked on *20,000 Leagues*, *Swiss Family Robinson*, and *Treasure Island*, among other films, used matte paintings to create the cave sequences for *Darby*. He also solved the movie's own unique conundrum— how to "shrink" human-sized actors to tiny leprechaun size—by employing a staging trick: forced perspective. Albert Sharpe, the actor playing Darby, was placed close to the camera; Jimmy O'Dea as King Brian stood four times further away from the camera as did Sharpe, creating the illusion that Darby was four times larger than the King. Of course, this solution necessitated building duplicate sets: a normal sized one for Darby and another four times larger for the King.

Perfect lighting was also crucial to the process. A massive number of lights—649 to be exact—were installed in the rafters of the new soundstage. These generated tremendous heat, enough to frequently suspend production. On one occasion, the shutdown extended well beyond the studio gates. When the new lights were first switched on, they caused a citywide blackout in Burbank!

Such hiccups aside, Ellenshaw's use of forced perspective created a masterful illusion in *Darby*

O'Gill and the Little People. The technique has been widely praised by modern directors like Steven Spielberg and Peter Jackson, who later employed it to great effect in his *Lord of the Rings* films. Disney released several more memorable live-action films in the succeeding years, including *The Absent-Minded Professor* and *Babes in Toyland*, before setting to work on arguably the most historic film ever shot on the Burbank lot: *Mary Poppins*.

Walt struggled for more than twenty years to secure the rights to the story against the strong objections of author P. L. Travers. Soon after the songwriting team of Richard and Robert Sherman joined the Disney staff in 1960, they received a gift of sorts: a copy of *Mary Poppins*. The "boys," as Walt referred to them, pored over it, picking out the chapters that they thought held the greatest potential. When they reported back to Walt with their now well-worn copy, he produced one of his own—with the very same chapters highlighted.

"When we read the *Mary Poppins* books, we were so impressed with the characters and the stories. They were wonderful, but there was no story line," Richard Sherman recalled. "It was a series of adventures. Mary Poppins flies in for no apparent reason and flies away again at the end. And they have these wonderful adventures, and certain things that stood out as being absolutely wonderful. And we wove them into a kind of a story."

For two and a half years, the Shermans labored over the script, only to learn that Disney

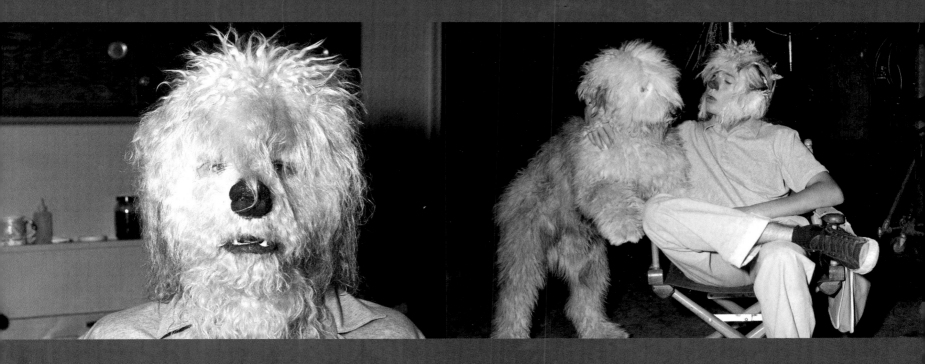

held the option to the book but not the film rights. The notoriously picky author soon visited the studio herself and summarily announced that she didn't like anything the brothers had written, according to Richard Sherman. Travers was then given thirty days to consider moving forward with the film; finally, on the very last day, she acquiesced . . .with one condition: Travers herself would serve as consultant.

Walt and his staff now took on the most crucial and vexing challenge in the entire production: finding the perfect Poppins. Mary Martin, Bette Davis, and Angela Lansbury were among the many stars considered until one night when, by happy coincidence, the Sherman brothers and screenwriter Don DaGradi all

happened to be home watching the same television program: *The Ed Sullivan Show*. On that night's show, a young talent named Julie Andrews performed "What Do the Simple Folk Do?" from the Broadway musical *Camelot* alongside Richard Burton.

The next morning, the trio burst into Disney's office to rave about Andrews. An intrigued Walt soon flew to New York to watch her in *Camelot* and decided she was, indeed, their *Mary Poppins*. After the show, he went backstage to convince her to take the part. "He started acting out the whole script of *Mary Poppins* right there in that small little room," Andrews said.

Filming the famous "Step in Time" rooftop dance for *Mary Poppins* (c. 1963).

Julie Andrews is prepped by special effects wizard Wathel Rogers for her "Spoonful of Sugar" duet with a cheerful robin in *Mary Poppins* (c. 1963).

But there was one other person who needed to be convinced: P. L. Travers, whose contract gave her final say over all aspects of the movie—including casting. Julie Andrews essentially needed to audition for the author. "I met her very briefly in London," Andrews recalled. "She, I think, was fond of me and approved of my doing *Poppins*. I know she said that I had the nose for it."

Finally, *Mary Poppins* was ready to start filming and Disney's soundstages were quickly transformed to scenes of Edwardian London. Andrews was beset by nerves, particularly when Director Robert Stevenson chose to shoot one of the biggest and most complicated scenes—the song "Jolly Holiday" on the first day. "I'd never made a movie before," she said, "and they were so tender with me. I was so scared, and I had no idea what I was doing."

Dick Van Dyke, who played the affable everyman Bert, found the dance sequences challenging since he had no professional training, according to choreographer Dee Dee Wood. For "Step in Time" rehearsals, a rudimentary version of the London rooftops set was built on the studio back lot adjacent to the *Zorro* village square. The cast spent weeks in grueling outdoor practices but ultimately executed the dance perfectly—twice! The reprise—which involved some of the more complicated portions of the routine like the smokestack elements—was required when filmmakers discovered scratches on the film master.

Mary Poppins, which opened in 1964, captured hearts the world over and earned Julie Andrews an Oscar for her portrayal of Mary Poppins. True to form, P. L. Travers was said to still have some notes following the film's premiere. Nearly fifty years later, the complicated relationship between the author and Walt would get a Disney live-action film of its own, 2013's *Saving Mr. Banks*.

Having proven his golden touch once more, Walt would keep his studio bustling with more animated and live-action features and new and increasingly diverse ventures, starting in the 1950s, like television and his new theme park, Disneyland.

Julie Andrews as Mary Poppins in the Cherry Tree Lane set, Stage Two.

CHAPTER 7

FROM ALICE TO ZORRO

Walt films a TV spot called "My Dad Walt Disney" (1957).

Soon after broadcast television debuted in 1934, Walt Disney took a break from *Snow White* for a trip to Camden, New Jersey. There, he and several other Hollywood executives watched a demonstration of the new medium by RCA head David Sarnoff. Many left the exhibition worried for their jobs: if people could be entertained from the comfort of their living room armchairs, why would they still flock to theaters?

But Walt, forever a champion of new technology, saw only potential in this burgeoning world. "There's a big, exciting period ahead of us, and I say it's television," he told biographer Pete Martin in a 1956 interview. "Television is an 'open sesame' to many things. I don't have to worry about going out and selling the theater man. I mean, I go right to the audience. I have a chance by getting there twenty-six times every year. I have a chance to have a pretty good batting average and not have to get in a rut."

His first tentative foray came in late 1944 when Disney joined the National Broadcasting Company (NBC) to develop *The World in Your Living Room*, a film *about* television. The project never made it to production, but preliminary research afforded the studio an invaluable education on all aspects of broadcasting.

Walt's interest in television would only intensify in the following years. Shortly after the end of World War II, he applied to the Federal Communications Commission for a television station license, announcing his plans to build a broadcasting studio on the Burbank lot. His brother Roy, so often the voice of financial reason, convinced him to withdraw the application. Roy also saw the great financial potential of television—both for recycling old films and making new ones with corporate sponsors—but Walt's plan was simply too expensive.

Ironically, the brothers' entry into the modern world of television came through the old-fashioned world of radio. Jack Webb, the creator of the *Dragnet* radio show, planned to convert his popular serial into a TV series and needed a place to film it. The Disneys agreed to build a soundstage—Stage Two—and rent it to Webb. *Dragnet* would film on the new stage from August 1952 through February 1955.

Disney's first foray into television, the TV special *One Hour in Wonderland*, was filmed in November 1950.

But even before that, by 1950, Walt was finished biding his time. Emboldened by a study the studio had commissioned titled "Television for Walt Disney Productions," Walt announced plans for Disney's first venture into broadcasting. It was a special, *One Hour in Wonderland*, an hour-long holiday program starring Edgar Bergen, Kathryn Beaumont, and Walt himself, that gave audiences a fanciful glimpse of the upcoming film *Alice in Wonderland*. It debuted on Christmas Day to impressive ratings, much to the delight of sponsor Coca-Cola. More importantly, the show gave Walt exactly what he craved—a direct relationship with the public to showcase his upcoming projects.

Disney followed up its first TV show with another special the following year, *The Walt Disney Christmas Show*, this time promoting *Peter Pan*. When this, too, was a hit, all three of the major television networks lobbied the studio to develop a series for their airwaves. Walt hoped to leverage that interest into an investment stake in the development of a Disneyland theme park, among other windfalls. "Every time I'd get to thinking of television, I would think of this park. And I knew that if I did anything like the park, that I would have some kind of a medium like television to let the people know about it," Walt explained.

"So I said, 'Well here's the way I'll get my park going. It's natural for me to tie in with television.' So it happened that I had sort of a say whether we went into television or not. I had a contract that said I had complete say of what

we produced. So I just sort of insisted that my Disneyland park be a part of my television show."

This plan proved harder than anticipated, however, as the network chiefs considered Walt's theme park concept a risky proposition. In the end, the fledgling American Broadcasting Company (ABC) agreed to loan Disney $500,000 and guaranteed another $4.5 million in loans. In return, ABC received a one-third ownership stake in Disneyland—*and* Walt's commitment to produce a weekly Disney television show on their network. It was, in business terms, a win-win: Walt got the capital he needed to complete Disneyland, and ABC secured a highly coveted production contract with the hit-making studio.

Disney's first series on ABC was the *Disneyland* anthology series, which Walt, as host, used to showcase the construction of his new "Magic Kingdom." Each week, audiences were treated to sneak peeks of exciting realms: Fantasyland, Adventureland, Frontierland, and Tomorrowland.

"He was very intense about his lead-ins," recalled Walt's daughter Diane Disney Miller. "He didn't particularly want to do them in the first place, *he* says, although he was kind of a ham; well, very much so, and a would-be actor in his youth. But he really took them seriously. What he really wanted to do was present to people what he was going to show them, and I think he did it in such a wonderful way because he really was so eager; he was so in love, he believed so much in what he was going to present."

In his book *Ears and Bubbles*, Mouseketeer Bobby Burgess describes watching Walt film his lead-ins for the program. "I loved seeing Mr. Disney," Burgess wrote, "and I would often sneak into the soundstage next door where he would film his intros for the *Disneyland* show. It was completely dark, and I'd watch this legend reading his cue cards with such natural warmth, just like he was somebody's favorite uncle."

Walt would sometimes use sections of the studio for his introductions, giving the public glimpses into the interiors of soundstages and studio buildings. The majority, though, were filmed on a set built to resemble his office on the

Walt Disney, with Director Robert Stevenson, on the set of the television show *I Captured the King of the Leprechauns* (c. 1958).

Fess Parker as Davy Crockett on the roof of the Alamo set, which was entirely enclosed inside Stage Three (c. 1956).

third floor of the Animation Building. To ensure authenticity, the set was dressed with various awards and mementos that would travel back and forth from office to "office."

The *Disneyland* anthology series also featured footage from the studio's feature film releases, which were broken into weekly installments, and all-new serialized stories like the instantly popular adventures of Davy Crockett. Director Norman Foster originally cast Buddy Ebsen as the heroic, rough-and-ready Crockett. But some staffers had misgivings about the choice and urged Walt to check out a bit player in the latest science fiction movie, *Them!* That actor, Fess Parker, spent only a minute on-screen, but that was ample time to convince Walt that Parker, not Ebsen, should be his Davy.

Ebsen was then switched to the role of trusty sidekick George Russel, a "demotion" he didn't take well initially—until he saw Parker as Crockett on-screen. Foster, whose lead casting choice was overruled by Walt, wasn't quite so gracious. He and Parker clashed often on the set, usually over Davy's personality. The director demanded a more boisterous Crockett, while Parker's portrayal was laid-back and thoughtful.

Walt's involvement in *Davy Crockett* extended well beyond casting. ABC gave Disney $100,000 per episode but, as usual, he prioritized quality over budget. The studio spent $700,000 on the first three episodes, with Walt dipping into his pockets to cover the cost overruns. They also shot on location in North Carolina and Tennessee, an unprecedented move for a TV show at the time. With an eye toward creative repackaging, Walt also demanded the series be shot in color, even though television was only broadcast in black and white. He eventually released episodes as two full-color feature films: *Davy Crockett, King of the Wild Frontier* (1955) and *Davy Crockett and the River Pirates* (1956).

The third episode of the TV series, *Davy Crockett at the Alamo*, marked longtime Disney staffer Marvin Davis's first turn as art director. After extensive research into the history and architecture of the famous San Antonio, Texas, mission where the battle occurred, Marvin designed a single elaborate set of it on Stage Three. "It was as close as I could make it," recalled Davis. "A few alterations were required

because we didn't have the size and space of the actual Alamo to do it in, but as far as the details and the feeling of it, it was quite accurate."

Construction of the set began in the fall of 1954. "The fort was built all the way around so we could shoot in any direction," Davis noted. "We built the upper level of the fort, the interior cells and offices, the commander's office—everything—where they would be in the actual fort. That way, when you were filming someone coming down the steps, you could actually follow them all the way down and right into the commander's office, or jail cell, or whatever. This gave a pretty good sense of realism rather than separating it as they usually do on a motion picture," he said.

Roughly the size of a football field, Disney's Alamo was at the time one of the biggest indoor sets ever built. The six-foot-thick walls of the faux adobe mission were only twenty-five feet from the interior walls of the soundstage. Once the working cannons were mounted on the wall, they were only inches from the backdrop. Davis and his crew also painted an enormous panoramic backdrop, offering the illusion of the vast Texas countryside beyond the walls of the fort.

Despite only airing three times during the first season of the Disneyland anthology, *Davy Crockett* was a wildly successful series with a bright future except for one slight problem—Davy dies heroically in the finale, at the Alamo. Walt solved this minor inconvenience by producing two more episodes about the "legend" of Davy Crockett: *Davy Crockett's Keelboat Race* and *Davy Crockett and the River Pirates*, both featuring the brash scoundrel Mike Fink as Davy's new nemesis. In all, Disney would produce only five hour-long episodes for the series, a fact that belies the tremendous cultural impact the show would have on a generation of children and parents alike.

On the heels of *Davy Crockett*, Walt chose a new hero for the anthology's "Frontierland" segments: Elfego Baca, a real-life gunman turned Old West lawyer. Foster was brought back to direct *The Nine Lives of Elfego Baca* with Robert Loggia cast as the lead. "To suddenly have the opportunity to be a hero in a Western endeavor by Walt Disney is like I'd died and went to

The Mouseketeers perform for Walt Disney during filming of *The Fourth Anniversary Show* (1957).

heaven," said Loggia. "I remember Walt saying, 'Can you ride, son?' I said, 'No, sir, but I can learn. I was a good athlete.' And he said, 'Okay.' And I got the accelerated course in drawing a gun and wearing a cowboy hat."

Once again, Walt spared no detail or expense on *Elfego Baca*. "Walt Disney spent so much money for a given show that he was losing money. There was no way to make it back, but he was such a stickler for doing it right," Loggia said.

The series shot on location in New Mexico, where the actual Elfego Baca lived. Walt wanted to use the actual churches and buildings, though this proved too costly, particularly when he upped the series order from two to ten. Production then moved to the studio's back lot, where a new, realistic Western street was built for a hefty $400,000 price tag. The street, located just north of the *Zorro* set, included multiple rows of facades, dirt streets with raised wooden sidewalks, a saloon, a bank, a hotel, an opera house, a jail, a stable, and just about every other old-fashioned edifice one would expect in Disney's versions of the Wild West.

Walt would use the back lot set for his next Western, *Texas John Slaughter*. The Walt Disney *Presents* (formerly *Disneyland*) series starring Tom Tryon ran a total of seventeen episodes, making it the longest-running series ever to air on the anthology program.

As part of Disney's deal with ABC, Walt created one of America's most fondly remembered television shows, the *Mickey Mouse Club*. The series would change the look of children's television and launch the careers of several of its young stars, including Annette Funicello, Tim Considine, Tommy Kirk, and Kevin Corcoran.

Shot mostly on Stage One, Walt originally modeled the *Mickey Mouse Club* after other "kid shows" popular in the 1950s, right down to the live studio audience. He soon ditched this idea in favor of a musical variety show with cartoons, newsreels, serialized stories, a revolving series of hosts, and, of course, a core group of multitalented young performers known as the "Mouseketeers."

Working with child actors who needed to balance school as well as rehearsals and filming posed certain logistical challenges for the producers, who split the group into three production groups: the "Red Team," "White Team," and "Blue Team." Two trailers — "The Little Red Schoolhouses" — were permanently parked in front of Stage One; they were for the Mouseketeers and the other young actors working on the lot.

During rare breaks, the kids used the studio's wide avenues and grassy areas for impromptu football games and games of tag. "On the north side of the cafeteria was a big lawn, and that's where we'd play baseball or football," recalled Burgess. "Ping-Pong was big then also, with tables set on the terrace beside the cafeteria."

The Mouseketeers needed to be on their best behavior at all times, a lesson reinforced during the first few days of production when Paul Petersen was let go for disruptive behavior, and Mickey Rooney's two sons, Tim and Mickey Jr., were fired for an unsanctioned, messy foray into the studio paint department. (Petersen would later find his way back into Disney's good graces and appear in 1967's *The Happiest Millionaire*.) But overall, the young actors served as models of professionalism and decorum, no surprise given that their mothers accompanied them to work every day. Walt originally allowed the women on the set, but a handful of pushy "stage mamas" got them relegated to the theater lobby, where they spent endless hours knitting, reading, or playing cards.

Around the time the *Mickey Mouse Club* hit the airwaves, Walt began work on another prized project. Three years earlier, he had obtained the television rights to Johnston McCulley's 1919 adventure novel *The Mark of Zorro* and pitched the series unsuccessfully to ABC as part of their development deal. As costs for his Disneyland theme park mounted in 1955, Walt again offered *Zorro* to the network, and this time they agreed.

Already beloved by radio and movie audiences, the masked swashbuckler would now make his first appearance on the small screen,

Walt on set with the Mouseketeers (1957).

Guy Williams as "Zorro the Fox," filming on the studio back lot (c. 1957).

and every Hollywood leading man lobbied for the part. For Guy Williams, Walt's eventual choice, it felt like destiny. Guy and his wife would often drive into the hills of Griffith Park and look down into the Disney back lot as *Zorro*'s sets were being built, according to his son, Guy Williams Jr. "'I'm going to get that role,'" the son said his dad would proclaim.

Walt planned to shoot *Zorro* on location in Mexico before deciding that building sets on the back lot—and shooting exterior scenes at local movie ranches—was far more practical. The "El Pueblo de Nuestra Señora de Los Angeles" was built first, according to the August 1957 *Zorro* newsletter, on a seven-acre space at the east end of the Burbank back lot. The set took six months to build and cost approximately $500,000.

Marvin Davis, along with collaborator Stan Jolley and their team, brought the same attention to detail to *Zorro* as he did to his *Davy Crockett* sets. The erected church was an exact replica of the original pueblo church located in downtown Los Angeles. The hinges on the huge

hand-hewn doors were actual wrought iron. Windows of hand-pounded iron were carefully cast out of special prop materials and painted to look like they'd been pounded by hammers. Many of the ornate wooden windows were genuine, from recently torn down early Spanish buildings. And every adobe brick was carefully antiqued with paint and putty to give the entire pueblo an aged and weathered appearance.

Actor Britt Lomond, who played the show's villainous Monastario, paid homage to Davis and his designers in his book *Chasing After Zorro*:

The appointment of these outstanding, artistically talented gentlemen to the *Zorro* series was a superb stroke of genius. The results of their collaboration on all of the *Zorro* sets, was magnificent. It was all there, complete and beautiful in authenticity and serviceability. As an actor, it is easy to give a good performance when everything around you has such superb authenticity to it.

Many of *Zorro*'s lavish exterior sets did not exist at all. The Mission San Juan Capistrano and Don Carlos's hacienda were matte paintings created by Peter Ellenshaw, and the exterior of the de la Vega hacienda, often seen as an

THE GOLDEN OAK RANCH

David Stollery and Tim Considine as "Spin and Marty" at the Golden Oak Ranch.

As 1920s audiences stampeded to movie theaters to watch the latest Westerns, Hollywood struggled with a unique challenge: how to re-create the wide-open expanses of the Old West. Studio back lots lacked both space and authenticity, while location filming was prohibitively expensive.

Disney, like many studios, turned to so-called "movie ranches." While filming the *Mickey Mouse Club*'s television serial *The Adventures of Spin and Marty* in 1955, Walt began leasing the historic Golden Oak Ranch in Placerita Canyon, which is approximately twenty-five miles north of the Burbank studio. The site was part of the Rancho San Francisco land grant, where gold was first discovered in California in 1842. More relevant to Walt, it was conveniently located in the nearby Santa Clarita Valley, a short drive from the studio.

Four years later, with Disney's outdoor filming needs rapidly increasing, Walt purchased the 315-acre ranch and began adding parcels. Today the ranch, now nine hundred acres in size, provides the studio with a multitude of natural settings: forests, meadows, woods, lakes, creeks, and waterfalls, as well as bridges, roads, and rural set buildings, along with a contemporary "Business District" and "Residential Street."

The iconic covered bridge at Disney's Golden Oak Ranch.

establishing shot for the show, only existed as artwork by Albert Whitlock.

The interior sets were often modified or redressed when temporary sets were required. The interior of the San Gabriel Winery, for example, later became the redecorated interior of the tavern. Both the Verdugo and Cornelio homes utilized the de la Vega hacienda set. All this redressing came at a price, literally: Davis's team spent $65,000 on furnishings and props for the various incarnations of the sets during the series' run.

Everything on *Zorro* was expensive, right down to the high-quality costumes and original music. Television shows in the 1950s never boasted original scores, but precedent—and budgets—were of little interest to Walt Disney. William Lava composed music for all seventy-eight episodes of the show, which had about fifteen minutes of music per episode—no small feat given that the series shot on an aggressive five-day production schedule. In total, each episode of *Zorro* cost about $78,000, which allowed for a final product that looked and felt more like films than television of the day. This fact wasn't lost on McCulley, *Zorro*'s creator, who visited the set often and praised the show's authenticity.

This realism extended even to *Zorro*'s frequent sword-fight scenes. Fred Cavens, a seventy-two-year-old master swordsman, trained the cast and choreographed the extravagant fight sequences, many of which took three to five hours to film. Cavens worked with virtually every leading man in TV and film in those days to teach them the art of wielding a sword, including famous swashbuckling stars of the time like Douglas Fairbanks Jr., Errol Flynn, and another Zorro, Tyrone Power. Luckily for him, Guy Williams had more experience than most. Two years earlier, Williams had dislocated his shoulder and broken an arm while filming a Universal picture. He had taken up fencing as part of his physical therapy, which came in mighty handy during his audition for the part.

Of course, swordplay was only one element of the action in *Zorro*. The scripts also called for elaborate, if not downright dangerous, stunts. Williams liked to do his own stunt work whenever possible, but the trickier ones, like

Guy Williams works out a fencing scene with fight choreographer Fred Cavens on the set of *Zorro* (1957).

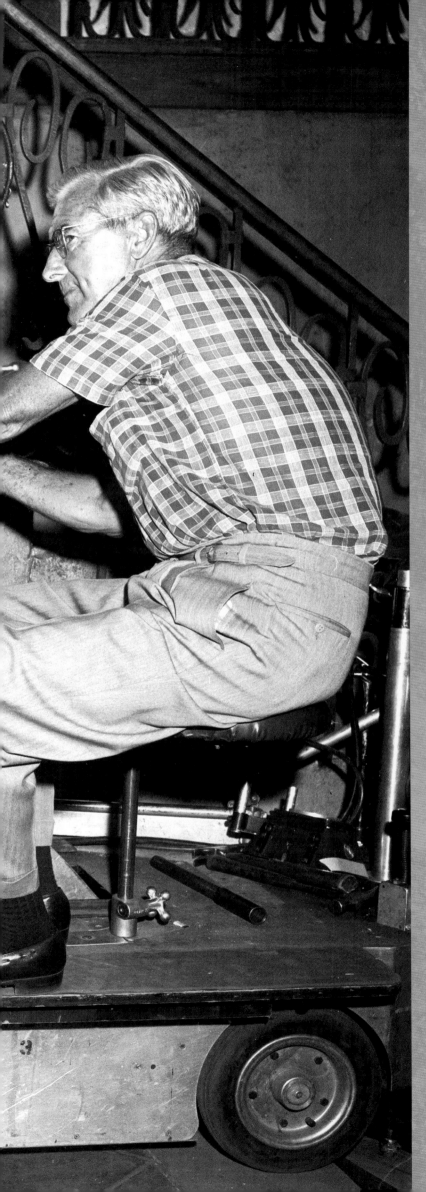

when Zorro needed to make an eight- or nine-foot jump, went to his double, Buddy Van Horn. "I was expendable, and he wasn't," Van Horn noted dryly. In fact, stunts were usually filmed on Fridays, which gave the stuntmen the weekend to recover if they sustained injuries.

Van Horn completed almost all his action scenes in full costume, including the sweeping cape that was both a hindrance and hazard when leaping from rooftops or onto horses and wagons. "The cape definitely became a problem," said Van Horn, "and sometimes I would shorten the cape up with some pins so I wouldn't step on it because I'd had that happen several times, and then the next thing that would hit the ground would be your head." As a result, observant viewers may have noticed a bit of a continuity issue in the show, as the cape would be shorter for Van Horn's stunts than they were for Williams's scenes.

While spared the dangerous stunts, Williams faced a "nearly equally" nerve-racking challenge—working out his Zorro accent in front of Walt himself. The boss made frequent appearances to the set during rehearsals. At the start of the series, Williams would find him standing just off camera and motioning for Guy to tone down the accent. Williams would make the necessary adjustment then look over again to find Walt gesturing for him to bring it up a little. When, one day, Walt ceased giving him cues, Williams said, "That's the accent I kept."

Zorro became a massive hit, propelling Williams to heartthrob status, even within the studio itself, as Mouseketeer Annette Funicello recalled: "For my sixteenth birthday, Walt Disney knew that I was crazy in love with Guy Williams. And [he] came to me one day with a script, and he said, 'How would you like to appear in *Zorro*?' And I said, 'You're kidding! Me?' And he said, 'Well, now that you're all grown-up, here's your script.' And it was such a thrill for me that Mr. Disney would think of such a wonderful birthday present."

Zorro's tremendous popularity capped an already impressive string of hits during Disney's first decade in television. More importantly, the studio's success vindicated Walt's faith in television's potential, as a way to connect directly with audiences and as a wellspring for ever-expanding arrays of programming.

Guy Williams on the set of *Zorro* (1957).

CHAPTER 8

BUILDING A KINGDOM

Walt with master matte artist Peter Ellenshaw and
his aerial map of Disneyland (1954).

"To all who come to this happy place: welcome. Disneyland is your land. Here, age relives fond memories of the past, and here youth may savor the challenge and promise of the future. Disneyland is dedicated to the ideals, the dreams, and the hard facts that have created America, with the hope that it will be a source of joy and inspiration to all the world."

With these words, Walt officially opened his first theme park on Sunday, July 17, 1955. Disneyland's dedication ceremony, televised live across the United States, fulfilled an ambition dating back to 1938, when Disney and his staff were still entrenched in the cramped Hyperion compound, according to Bob Jones, who worked in the Model Department.

In a 1956 interview, Walt recalled, "When I built the studio over there [in Burbank], I thought well, gee, we ought to have a three-dimensional thing that people could actually come and visit. They can't visit our studio because the rooms are small. It's too disrupting to have anybody on the lot. So I had a little dream for Disneyland adjoining the studio."

Jones said Walt enlisted staffers to assist with the park project as far back as 1938, even before the move to new quarters in Burbank. "Walt came and [gave us] a direct assignment. They were building this studio, a big studio. He had earmarked the southeast corner of this lot, two acres, as a little kiddie park. And for six weeks we worked on this kiddie park, just drawing sketches, and Walt would come in every night about five o'clock [with] sketches.

"Sometimes we would work until six or seven on it," Jones added. "We had a little mine train ride, we had Geppetto's workshop, a little picnic place; then we had the Dwarfs' cottage. And it was just a very simple thing, but that was really—as far as I know—the beginning of Disneyland."

Even while busy with other projects, Walt would continue to brainstorm and think of potential new attractions for a family park not even on the drawing board, including one reflecting his newfound interest in miniatures and scale-model live steam trains. "He was thinking of putting in a little half-inch scale railroad that would zigzag its way over to the studio lot," Animator Ward Kimball said. "The track would go through the different soundstages so the riding tourists could see how films were made."

In 1941, Walt found a way to give fans a peek behind Disney's hallowed gates—at least virtually. *The Reluctant Dragon*, a fanciful live-action/animation "documentary," treated audiences to an insider's tour of the new Burbank lot. Almost immediately, the studio was inundated with letters from children—and adults—wanting to visit the home of Mickey Mouse and Snow White.

The plan for Disneyland slowly took shape. Walt first conceived of a "Mickey Mouse Park" across from the studio, where fans could see beloved Disney characters in their fantasy surroundings. To the surprise of no one, his ideas became increasingly grander and more extravagant, no longer a kiddie park now but a full-fledged amusement complex complete with scale-model live steam trains. Walt began a search for a space big enough to accommodate his park, ultimately laying claim to a parcel of land thirty-eight miles south of Burbank, in Anaheim.

As his vision for the theme park expanded, Walt enlisted more Disney staffers to help. Disney artist and Imagineer Herb Ryman remembered being called into work on a

continued on page 114

A rendering of "Mickey Mouse Park"—an early incarnation of the park that opened in 1955 as Disneyland.

WED staff members Dick Irvine, C. V. Wood, Bill Cottrell, and Nat Winecoff view a model of the *Mark Twain Riverboat* with Walt in 1954.

Saturday in 1952. "When I got to the studio, Walt said, 'Hi, Herb. We have a new project. It's sort of an amusement park.' I asked Walt what he was going to call it and he said, 'Disneyland.'"

Walt then proceeded to give Ryman a detailed overview of the park and told him Roy O. was traveling to New York that Monday to start raising funds. But first, they needed a concrete plan. "The bankers," Walt surmised, "don't have any imaginations."

So began the historic weekend in which Walt and Ryman hunkered down over a drawing board to create the first detailed map of Disneyland. Their whimsical, beautifully rendered drawing— remarkable for its accurate depiction of the final layout of the park—was instrumental in convincing ABC to partner with Disney. It now resides in the Walt Disney Imagineering Art Library, arguably the most valuable and significant piece of art in the collection.

As with the studio's expansion into television, Roy O. initially opposed the park as too risky a proposition. Walt found a way, however, to assuage his brother's doubts in the unlikeliest of places: his budding train hobby. Recently, Disney had established a private company, the Walt Disney Miniature Railroad Company, through which he sold drawings of his backyard locomotive (the *Lilly Belle*), parts castings for engines and cars, and even castings of the train's miniature potbellied stove. By 1952, Walt's little company was incorporated as WED Enterprises, Inc., an acronym for Walter Elias Disney. Incorporating allowed Walt to legally protect the valuable Disney name and finance his theme park without mortgaging the studio's future.

"Well, WED is, you might call it my backyard laboratory, my workshop away from work" said Walt in a 1964 interview. "It served a purpose in that some of the things I was planning, like Disneyland for example...it's pretty hard for banking minds to go with it...so I had to go ahead on my own and develop it to a point where they could begin to comprehend what I had on my mind."

Marvin Davis and former Disney staffer Richard Irvine, both art directors from 20th Century Fox, joined WED Enterprises in

Walt views schematics during the construction of the *Columbia Sailing Ship* on a studio soundstage (1957).

Disney Imagineer Ken Anderson guides the layout of the track for Disneyland's *Peter Pan's Flight* attraction (1955).

early 1953 and, with Walt as the ever-present supervisor, set to work on the new park. Irvine, among others, talked his boss out of plans to hire an architectural firm, Pereira & Luckman, to create the overall layout and design.

Disneyland didn't need architects, they insisted, it needed magic, and who created magic better than Walt Disney and his staff? Walt needed no further convincing; by 1954, WED's staff had grown to include designers, architects, writers, artists, sculptors, engineers, special effects artists, model makers, and masters of every other discipline necessary to bring the Disneyland dream to life.

The task ahead seemed Herculean, especially given the planned opening date: July 17, 1955. But the ever-fastidious Walt refused to sacrifice quality. He insisted that scale models, not just conceptual drawings, be created to better gauge the size, scope, and design of each project. "When Walt was designing a new attraction, he wanted to see it as a model. As he said one time,

'Renderings lie, but a scale model does not,'" noted Imagineer Rolly Crump.

The studio's Model Shop became a critical early stop in Disneyland's development process. And despite Walt's best efforts to account for future growth when building the Burbank studio, the unit was more or less homeless. Model makers Fred Joerger, Harriet Burns, and Wathel Rogers were crammed into a boxcar alongside the machinists outside the studio's entrance on Buena Vista Street.

"Back then," said Burns, "everything we had was junk! Sometimes we'd set up a sort of plywood table to show the models on. My 'desk' was a table-saw with a piece of plywood over it, and I had an old bent-up stool. So, when we needed to use the table-saw, it would take Wathel and Fred to lift the plywood off, and we'd make the needed cut, and then put the plywood back down. This was just like working with your neighbor in your garage. It was very funny."

The construction of passenger cars for the *Santa Fe and Disneyland Railroad* inside a studio soundstage (1955).

Imagineers Fred Joerger, Claude Coats, and Harriet Burns create a "Candy Mountain" model for the *Storybook Land Canal Boats* attraction at Disneyland (1957).

The unpleasant working conditions didn't deter Walt from visiting the boxcar—almost every day. "When Walt got up to his eyeballs in company politics," said Burns, "he'd tell his secretary, Dolores Voght, 'I'm going to go take a walk on the back lot,' meaning that he would come visit us. Then he could relax. It was like his toy shop." Under his watchful eye, Burns and her fellow Imagineering pioneers created models for early attractions like Sleeping Beauty Castle; the *Mark Twain Riverboat*; Main Street, U.S.A.; and the Tahitian Terrace restaurant in Adventureland.

Separate six- to eight-inch Sleeping Beauty Castle models were created by artists Herb Ryman and Eyvind Earle (who was also a director). Earle chose a black, red, and gold color scheme, while Ryman painted his model in pastels. "Walt decided to go with the one Herbie [Ryman] did, with pastels. He felt it would look better against the blue sky that way," Burns recalled. She and Joerger then handcrafted a larger, detailed model of plywood and Masonite, with balsa wood turrets. Walt would frequently use this model to promote the new park, especially on his *Disneyland* anthology series.

The superstructure of the *Mark Twain* is constructed on a studio soundstage (1955).

One of the shop's early assignments was a model of a model in actuality, according to Burns. Walt assigned her, Joerger, and Rogers to build a temporary attraction called *Storybook Land* with scale-sized villages, homes, and castles for many of Disney's most beloved fairy-tale characters. Walt told them, "We can do this little ride, and it will be filler at the moment. Later on we can take it out and put something else there."

Temporary or not, the team spared no details: the attraction's church boasted elaborate stained glass windows, the rain gutters were soldered copper, and even the weather vanes featured intricate scenes, like a fox chasing a rabbit. "Nobody could really see it," Burns said, "but Walt knew it was there—that was the good part." *Storybook Land* quickly became a guest favorite at Disneyland, earning the attraction a permanent place—well, minus the weather vanes. "I don't think [the weather vanes] lasted very long on *Storybook Land* because the gardeners would knock them off," Burns complained.

With Disneyland's opening fast approaching, Walt made another unusual request: he wanted life-sized, walk-around representations of the Disney characters, most notably Mickey and Minnie Mouse. "Walt asked us to do some of those early heads simply because he didn't know who else to ask!" Burns remembers. "So, there

was a gal in Ink and Paint—I believe she did one, and I did Pluto and Goofy. I was not from Animation, and they shouldn't have had me do it, but there was nobody else!" Burns said.

"We had pieces of fur cloth, and we had access to Frank Millington and the Drapery Department next door," she added. "Frank would let us use anything that we needed. I did the heads in clay . . . and then we had a product called 'celastic.' It was a canvas impregnated in a plastic that you dipped in a solvent, which was ether, acetone, and other things. Of course, everything was toxic as heck, but we didn't know it! Then we padded [the inside]. They were heavy and crude. . . . But that was all we could do in the opening weeks. Eventually they got a costume department that did heads much better."

Meanwhile, in another bustling corner of the studio, Disneyland's rides were nearing completion, starting with Frontierland's *Stage Coach* in 1954. "When Walt first started talking about those stagecoaches, people advised him not to bother with real leather seats or painstakingly carved woodwork," Imagineer John Hench recalled. "They said people would just carve their initials in the wood and rip the leather anyway. Walt contended that people would [want] something well done, a work of art. You might say he 'compromised' to this

Imagineer Harriet Burns with Walt in the studio Model Shop (1955).

Walt rides aboard the newly built Disneyland *Stage Coach* in it's trial run about the studio lot (1953).

extent: he insisted only on two things—complete authenticity and perfection!"

The *Stage Coach* attraction ignited enthusiasm around the studio, and other completed projects would soon follow, including *Snow White's Adventures, Mr. Toad's Wild Ride,* and *Peter Pan's Flight.* Designer Bill Martin and artist Ken Anderson developed these so-called Fantasyland "dark rides," using vehicles built by an outside engineering company, Arrow Development of Mountain View, California.

"Viewing the film [tied to an attraction] was part of the design process," said Martin. "I made the track layout to start with, but we went through storyboards galore. Since the point was to convert Walt's cartoon films to rides in Fantasyland, those dark rides were developed from the original four-by-eight-foot storyboards and concept sketches made for the animated films."

The team frequently "borrowed" Animation Department artists to help out. "I had a break in my background work where I wasn't busy, so I got to do the model for the *Mr. Toad* attraction," remembered Claude Coats. "I painted it from Ken [Anderson's] sketches, and I painted it in black light; [it's] the first time I'd had any

experience in black light. Later, Walt came around to tell us that the scenic company [Grosh Studios] that was painting the other dark rides for the park would not be available. 'They can only get *Peter Pan* and *Snow White* done, so you guys do it.' So, having painted cel-sized backgrounds for twenty years, I went from a twelve-inch-high format to sets that were eighteen feet high."

The attractions were then mocked-up on studio soundstages because the prefabricated buildings that would house them hadn't been made yet. "Many of the rides were built at the studio, disassembled, and transported to the Anaheim park. The superstructure of the *Mark Twain* was entirely built on Stage Three, torn down, and rebuilt on the hull in the Rivers of America," Anderson said. "Walt wanted these rides close by, where he could keep close supervision on them. None like them had ever been built before, so the designers and builders were experimenting all the way."

Designer Marvin Davis said the *Peter Pan* attraction filled an entire building with "the overhead rails and the cars, and the dips and the swirls. This was something new, too. I don't think there had ever been an overhead-suspended ride in any amusement park. [And Walt] was the first

119

NEL Nº13

Scenic flats for *Mr. Toad's Wild Ride* being painted at the studio (1955).

one to go on them. Just like a little kid. He'd get off and giggle. Or, if he didn't like it too well, his eyebrow would go up and he would say, 'Well, goddamnit, fix this thing and let's get this show on the road.'"

Plans didn't always proceed smoothly, according to Anderson. The *Mr. Toad* attraction, for example, was built on flats. When sections of the wall, floor, and track were dismantled and trucked to the park for reassembly, he discovered the plans were sixteen inches off. Luckily, the attraction was eighteen inches smaller than the building, which meant the problem could be fixed, though not without some difficulty. Anderson joked that fixing the flats was "somewhat akin to building a house of cards with each card weighing five hundred pounds."

Walt and his team also squabbled with local labor unions that were miffed about the attractions being built in Burbank rather than locally in Orange County (where Anaheim is located). "We built the things here. We had the Hollywood know-how. When we'd built the ride

at the studio, it would be transported by truck to Disneyland," said Anderson. "And we'd discover that the labor unions in Orange County thought this was unfair. One ride was all finished and painted at the studio, and when we got it to Anaheim it was arbitrarily sandblasted and had to be repainted" by local laborers.

Transforming Walt's fanciful ideas into physical attractions of wood, steel, and wires often posed unique challenges as was certainly the case with *Autopia*, according to studio machinist Roger Broggie. "Walt's idea was young kids could learn to drive safely on the freeway by driving these automobiles on this safe pattern called *Autopia*. We built thirty-six automobiles in the first group of cars, two lines of eighteen each, and we tested them at the studio. My kids rode them at the studio; thought we had a car that was a riot. Then in the first ten days, we reduced the count from thirty-six to six. And instead of driving safely and learning how to drive automobiles, they took it as a crash program . . . crash one another," Broggie ruefully observed.

Walt inspects the restoration of a vintage circus wagon for the *Mickey Mouse Club Circus* at Disneyland (1955).

Walt explains his *Audio-Animatronics* dinosaur eggs to a studio visitor (1963).

The *Autopia* cars became a "bumper car" sensation on the back lot, particularly with young Mousketeers and Kirk Douglas's sons, who would visit their father on the set of *20,000 Leagues Under the Sea*. The trend would only intensify following *Autopia*'s installation at Disneyland, necessitating redesigns and enhancements in 1959, 1964, and 1968. In a 1979 interview with Disney archivist Dave Smith, Broggie noted, "We today are on [the] Mark 8. We've had eight revisions of designs, complete design changes, eight times, all the result of this constant impact. In other words, we've destroyed seven generations of automobiles."

The park would, of course, open as scheduled in July of 1955, but those who expected the attractions to always be the same, without any changes, didn't know Walt. "Disneyland will never be completed. It will continue to grow," Walt once said. By the spring of 1958, the Machine Shop, where the studio's huge original animation production cameras had been built and maintained, was reapportioned expressly to that end.

"I was still working special effects at the studio," Broggie remembered. "Walt said, 'You're off of this special effects work here.

Walt and two friends destined for the new *Jungle Cruise* attraction at Disneyland (1955).

Staff members carry a mechanized *Jungle Cruise* hippo from the soundstage where it was constructed (1955).

A wood mock-up of the interior of a Disneyland *Submarine Voyage* attraction vehicle.

Now we're going to turn this machine shop into a manufacturing facility for Disneyland.'" Thereafter, most of the park's boats. trams, streetcars—even the steam locomotives and original *Monorail* system—were designed by studio engineers, to say nothing of the mechanized figures for attractions like *Great Moments with Mr. Lincoln* and *"it's a small world."*

The Machine Shop staff, housed in the Technical Engineering and Manufacturing (T.E.A.M.) Building, soon ran out of space, and submarines, flying elephants, caterpillars, and carousel horses were overrunning the soundstages and back lot areas. Numerous attractions, however, including *Walt Disney's Enchanted Tiki Room, Haunted Mansion, General Electric's Carousel of Progress,* and *"it's a small world,"* continued to be mocked up at the Burbank studio, for Walt's inspection. "It must have been quite a sight for movie studio visitors to find the surrounding streets filled with *Autopia* cars, railroad cars and locomotives, animated animals, and all sorts of 'gags' under construction" said Imagineer Bob Gurr.

Walt shows his newly constructed *Monorail* to a guest on the studio back lot (c. 1958).

Testing tank for the *Submarine Voyage* attraction vehicles on the back lot. The Ink and Paint Building is visible in the background (1958).

Several new "E-ticket" attractions were introduced to Disneyland by the late 1950s, including 1959's *Submarine Voyage*, whose vessels had been tested on the back lot. "We did a half-shell mock-up to see how it would work," said Gurr, "then dug a hole outside the Machine Shop and placed a big concrete tank and a plate glass window in it. The hole was big enough to drop the entire mock-up into it, and we could look through the portholes at the plate glass and water behind it. We were able to work out the animation for the fish and so forth. Roger Broggie's Machine Shop crew did all the mechanical work for the sub ride, and that tank was there for years."

Disney engineers also completed the *Monorail* on the lot after an outside company, Standard Carriage Works, failed to meet its deadlines, according to Gurr. "I had four jobs running on top of one another [*Matterhorn, Autopia, Submarine Voyage*, and the *Monorail*], and I went completely nuts! And then, while they were fabricating the *Monorail* trains at Standard Carriage Works, they got so far behind that Roger Broggie pulled the whole job out of that professional factory and threw it into the studio! He put it into a soundstage [Stage Three] and told me, 'Bob, you are now the production manager,'" he recalled.

With their deadline looming, Gurr went so far as to cordon off the soundstage to keep "lookie-loos" away, including, quite accidentally, Walt himself: "He came by one day with Mickey Clark, his 'finance guy,' and Mickey had an envelope. As the guys walked off, Mickey handed me the envelope and said, 'Walt doesn't understand how you do this, but here.' I went back in and opened it up and there was a thousand dollars in there. I thought to myself how much Walt wanted the *Monorail* finished, but while I had the rope up, he wouldn't come in there."

Gurr and his team would, of course, meet their deadline, creating the sleekly futuristic yet classic-looking red Mark I *Monorail*. Vice President Richard Nixon dedicated the *Monorail* during a live televised ribbon cutting on June 14, 1959, then rode it around the park with Walt and his family.

Two years later, WED Imagineers began developing an innovative new technology with far-reaching implications for the park: *Audio-Animatronics*, a term it would later be called. They were lifelike robotic representations of animals and people that could move, sing, and even talk. Several American companies expressed interest and petitioned WED to design attractions featuring this technology for them for their exhibitions and pavilions at the

1964–1965 New York World's Fair. Walt agreed, thrilled at the prospect of experimenting at someone else's expense and knowing the attractions could later be installed at Disneyland. The New York World's Fair also afforded him the chance to gauge the feasibility and appeal of an East Coast version of Disneyland.

WED Enterprises became the most active independent designer for the international exposition, and Disney's Burbank studio was once again ground zero. The state of Illinois's *Great Moments with Mr. Lincoln* attraction, featuring an amazingly lifelike Abraham Lincoln, was built in the studio's Machine Shop; the Ford Pavilion's *Magic Skyway* attraction, a prototype similar to what would become the *PeopleMover* attraction in Tomorrowland, was built on the southeast corner of the studio's back lot.

There was also Pepsi-Cola and UNICEF's joint *"it's a small world"* attraction, which was entirely mocked up on one of the studio's soundstages, and *General Electric's Carousel of Progress*, which boasted full-scale sets constructed at the studio and was later featured on *Walt Disney's Wonderful World of Color* TV show on NBC. Walt and his team also found time to create their first Disneyland attraction featuring *Audio-Animatronics*. The attraction, *Walt Disney's Enchanted Tiki Room*, which opened in 1963, was a seventeen-minute tropical show with more than two hundred realistic-looking robotic birds, flowers, and tiki gods that talked, chanted, and whistled.

Burns recounted a memorable discussion during the construction of *Great Moments with Mr. Lincoln*: "In the shop, we had an early version of the head for Lincoln. I recall several of us were sitting around the plywood table discussing it. There was John Hench, Dick Irvine, Fred [Joerger], and myself. Walt said, 'Hmm…we can call it…anima…anima…Animatronics! We can combine electronics and animation! It will be called Animatronics.'

"And everybody was mumbling all these words together," Burns said. "Then Art Director Vic Green said, 'Yes, but there's sound in there, too.' Walt said, 'Well, that would be audio…' And so they added the word *Audio*

Walt presents robin and parrot *Audio-Animatronics* birds to Canadian Broadcasting Corporation host Fletcher Markle.

to *Animatronics*. Walt liked that. But I remember all of them saying these funny words together and combining them. Then Walt said, 'and we can have Lincoln be our first Audio-Animatronics character!'"

A huge admirer of the sixteenth president, Walt was particularly proud of the progress on *Great Moments with Mr. Lincoln*. He even showed off his animatronic version to gossip columnist Hedda Hopper during her June 1963 trip to the studio. Hopper, in her notes, recalled entering through a door that said, NO ADMITTANCE—THIS DOOR MUST BE KEPT LOCKED. There, she wrote, "sat Mr. Lincoln. The two fellows working there heated him up and he began to speak—with frown, mouth movements, turning head, eyes you'd swear were real."

Hopper was duly impressed with "President Lincoln," and the way he could move 364 different ways. In her notes, she also mentioned spotting something else of interest during her guided tour: "In the room was an umbrella that had a sign, 'DO NOT TOUCH.' It was topped by a parrot head that actually talks to Mary Poppins. The boss touched it and showed [me] how it moved its mouth."

Disney's production team was equally secretive about the Ford Magic Skyway project. "When we started on the World's Fair," Burns said, "we began by doing the model of the Ford Pavilion at the studio. We were told not to tell anybody what we were doing. We had built our wall further up—one story up. Of course, people could still look over it if they were really determined to, but they didn't want Chevrolet or anyone finding out what Ford was doing.

"So we built that wall up and had real good locks put on," Burns continued. "Roy Merchant [head of security] was allowed to come in, and the firemen had to come in once a week. When they came, they would ask us, 'What's that building?' But we wouldn't tell them. I'd tease them about it! Finally, I told them, 'We are building a new hotel for Disneyland—and I'm

The revolutionary new *Audio-Animatronics* figure of Abraham Lincoln rises up to a standing position.

Walt poses with baby dinosaur *Audio-Animatronics* figures created for the 1964–1965 New York World's Fair (1964).

going to be the madam!'"

Amid the chaos of the World's Fair projects, the Model Shop team learned they'd soon be moving to WED's new facilities a few miles away. It was, by all accounts, a necessary transition. By the mid-1960s, the Burbank studio strained to accommodate the production needs of their animated and live movies, television programs, Disneyland projects, and now the World's Fair attractions. "We have to have more room!" exclaimed Walt. "The World's Fair is not the Disney Studio—it's WED. We are just going to have to separate and get off the lot."

In 1965, Walt discovered all the space the company would need—for the time being anyway—at the Grand Central Industrial Park in neighboring Glendale. WED's departure began an exciting new chapter for what would eventually become known as Walt Disney Imagineering, even while it ended an era of incredible energy and activity at the Burbank

studio. On any given day, a visitor to the lot might bump into one of Hollywood's most famous actors, stroll past a giant movie or TV stage set of a far-off locale, or spot a startlingly real reproduction of anything from a U.S. president to a zebra, and a submarine to a spaceship.

The 1950s and 1960s were Disney's seminal age of wizardry and wonder, an eye-rubbing, waking dream from which the studio would abruptly awaken on December 15, 1966, when Walt died at St. Joseph's Hospital, just across the street from his beloved lot. Five years later, weeks after the opening of Walt Disney World in Florida, Roy O. would pass on December 20, 1971. The Disney brothers were gone; it was the end of an era, but not the end of the magic.

CHAPTER 9

WHAT WOULD WALT DO?

The Animation Building "stands in as Medfield College for 1975's *The Strongest Man in the World.*

In the wake of Walt's death in late 1966 and Roy's passing a few years later, one question was often raised around the studio: *What would Walt do?* Paradoxically, this mantra meant to inspire became something of an albatross for Walt Disney Productions.

There was, quite simply, no way to replace Walt's creativity and intuition, as well as the fearlessness and risk-taking that would allow Disney to thrive in the ever-changing entertainment world of the 1970s. The staff worried constantly about straying too far from Walt Disney's vision, and a resulting creative paralysis would plague the studio for more than a decade. The once lively and thriving Walt Disney Studios now seemed sleepy and somber, and while it would release several memorable animated and live-action films during this period—*Bedknobs and Broomsticks, Pete's Dragon, Freaky Friday, The Apple Dumpling Gang,* and *Tron* among them—surefire hits came with far less frequency.

Perhaps the most noteworthy—and profitable—film of this era was based on the story "Car-Boy-Girl," by Gordon Buford. The movie's producers would test-drive several different titles, including *Beetlebomb, Thunderbug,* and *The Magic Volksy,* before settling on the one which would permeate the cultural zeitgeist of a generation: *The Love Bug.*

The film's early stages of development sadly coincided with the last days of Walt's illness. Around that time, popular Disney actor Dean Jones recalled giving Walt a script he had optioned about the first sports car in America: "I said this would be good for us to make. [Walt] said, 'Dean, I read it … I've got a better car story for you.'" That story was "Car-Boy-Girl" and Jones would ultimately star as down-on-his-luck race car driver Jim Douglas.

Studio executives found the story charming and delightful and soon assembled the creative team behind *Mary Poppins* to lead the project, with Robert Stevenson directing, Bill Walsh producing and writing, and Don DaGradi as the story man. Their first challenge? Picking just the right car for the iconic title role.

"They had a casting call for cars," Jones recalled, "maybe close to a dozen cars lined up on the Walt Disney Studios lot one day" with contenders including a Toyota, a Fiat, a Volvo, an MG, and a Volkswagen. The producers parked the vehicles outside during lunch and watched employees' reactions as they passed. With most of the cars, the staff would give a quick, admiring glance or maybe kick the tires, but they treated the VW differently, reaching out to pet it like an amiable dog, sometimes even talking to it.

"It was an unpretentious car. It was very real, what-you-see-is-what-you-get. There was an honesty there," Jones recalled. His costar, Buddy Hackett, said, "I loved that car, and when I talked to the car, when I touched the car, it was like a friend."

It was Hackett who inadvertently inspired the Love Bug's name when writer and producer Walsh caught Buddy's stand-up act in Las Vegas. As part of the act, Hackett, in a thick German accent, told a story of his visit to a ski school. The instructors were "Franz, Hans, and Fritz, to which Buddy quipped, "If you ain't got a Herbie, I ain't going." Walsh loved the bit and soon after, Herbie was born.

Released in 1969, *The Love Bug* offered audiences the perfect blend of comedy, heart, and adventure. It topped the box office for 1969 and became Disney's second highest grossing film ever after (at that point) *Mary Poppins.*

The Apple Dumpling Gang films on Western Street (c. 1974).

Angela Lansbury, as apprentice witch Eglantine Price, films an outdoor scene on the studio back lot for *Bedknobs and Broomsticks* (c. 1970).

A.R.P. SHELTER →

Disney's 1971 musical fantasy *Bedknobs and Broomsticks* began as an insurance policy of sorts against the variable moods of *Mary Poppins* author P. L. Travers. As Travers wrung her hands endlessly over selling her story to Disney, Walt gave his creative team—the Sherman brothers, Bill Walsh, and Don DaGradi—two of Mary Norton's books: *The Magic Bed-Knob; or, How to Become a Witch in Ten Easy Lessons* and *Bonfires and Broomsticks*.

The team immediately began adapting the stories into a musical feature with underwhelming results: Walt reportedly fell asleep when the Shermans played some of their early songs at a pitch meeting. The project was then shelved because Travers finally gave the green light for *Mary Poppins*, and the team's focus shifted shifted away from Norton's work. Beginning in 1969, the Shermans spent two years on the film, and even resurrected the seafaring song "The Beautiful Briny," which was originally written for *Poppins*.

Though set in World War II-era England,

Bedknobs and Broomsticks was, remarkably, shot entirely at the Disney Studios. Outdoor sets, including the hamlet of Pepperinge Eye and Miss Price's quaint seaside cottage, were constructed on the back lot, while the memorable scenes of the medieval army laying siege to Nazi invaders and the extravagant three-block replica of London's iconic Portobello Road occupied the studio's massive soundstages. The "Portobello Road" sequence featured two hundred extras and performances by numerous veterans of vaudeville, silent films, and early talkies.

Despite a grand budget, Academy Award–winning visual effects, and a stellar cast (including Angela Lansbury as magical mistress Eglantine Price), *Bedknobs and Broomsticks* performed poorly at the box office. The movie would, however, become a family favorite with Disney enthusiasts in the years to follow.

In November 1977, the studio released another live-action/animated musical, *Pete's Dragon*, featuring popular actors Helen Reddy, Mickey

Through the use of the sodium-vapor process, Pete (Sean Marshall) "rides" Elliott the dragon up to the lighthouse where Nora (Helen Reddy) looks out to sea.

The fishing village of Passamaquoddy—an elaborate *Pete's Dragon* set on the studio back lot (c. 1970).

Rooney, and Shelley Winters. Newcomer Sean Marshall as Pete faced the enormous task—literally and figuratively—of bringing Elliott the dragon convincingly to life. "It was a real challenge to work with someone who wasn't really there," Marshall said of his cartoon costar.

Once again, the creative team turned to Disney's back lot, transforming old Western sets into the film's seaside village of Passamaquoddy. About thirty buildings received makeshift face-lifts—and eight more were built—to accommodate the various interiors and exteriors needed for the production. The crew actually

built the movie's iconic lighthouse off-site, on the Point Buchon seaside bluff in nearby Morro Bay. Its large Fresnel-style lighthouse lens produced a beacon that shone eighteen to twenty-four miles into the Pacific Ocean, requiring special permission from the U.S. Coast Guard, so as not to confuse ships at sea. Locals still refer to the area as "Disney Point," even though the lighthouse itself was dismantled years ago.

The studio, hoping for another *Mary Poppins*-sized hit, was disappointed upon the film's release in 1977. *Pete's Dragon* grossed an anemic $18 million though, like *Bedknobs and*

Special effects filming of the flying-bed sequence in *Bedknobs and Broomsticks*—through the use of the sodium-vapor process (c. 1970).

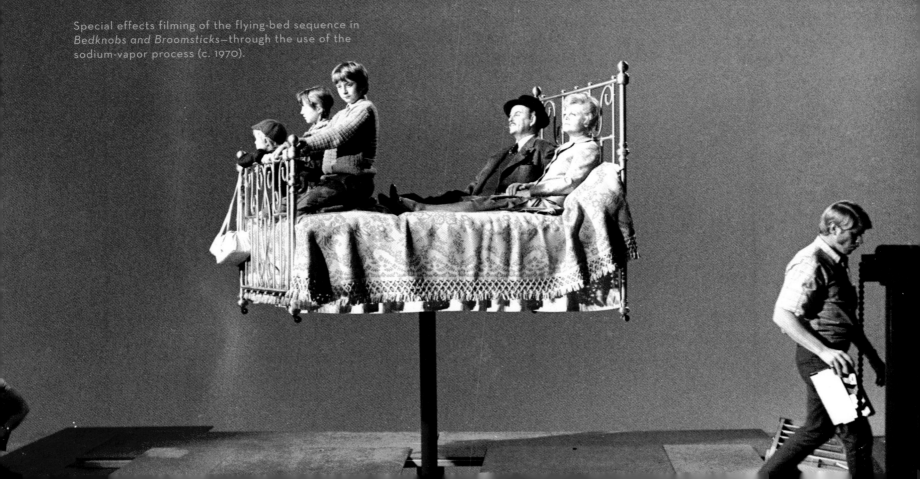

Broomsticks, it would in hindsight be reappraised as a classic of the era.

Ironically, Disney's era of creative stasis would produce one of the most groundbreaking movies in its history. A derivative of the word "elecTRONic," *Tron* was a science fiction parable that took place entirely within a computer.

"At the time, Disney was kind of considered old-fashioned. It wasn't contemporary," said Dick Cook, former chairman of the Walt Disney Studios. "A lot of the other studios were doing projects that were, frankly, more exciting. So, when *Tron* came along, it was met with a lot of anticipation by the younger people at the studio, and I think the older generation was wondering, 'What in the world is this all about? What are we doing?' and had no clue about what it was going to be because it was so far ahead of its time."

Tron, which was created and directed by Steven Lisberger, told the story of a young genius (played by Jeff Bridges) who hacks into his company's computer system and gets transported to a digital dimension where he must fight for his survival. This was in the days before desktop computers, cellular phones, and the Internet, when according to Lisberger, "people genuinely feared computers and they only existed as mainframes."

"Every one of us is in that computer somewhere, whether it's because of our driver's license or social security or income tax," he said. "When we did the film, the feeling we had about cyberspace was that it was this new frontier and that there was unlimited potential ... there was this sense of unbridled optimism."

Lisberger sought to capture both the apprehension and enthusiasm of the burgeoning digital revolution, starting with *Tron*'s tagline: A WORLD INSIDE THE COMPUTER WHERE MAN HAS NEVER BEEN. NEVER BEFORE NOW. But for a movie about modern technology, *Tron* was decidedly low-tech. "We had no computers on the set of *Tron*, and probably your cell phone has more computing power in it than we had on the whole movie," Lisberger would recall years later.

The electric, illuminated techno-glow of the computer world required frame-by-frame

Tron director Steven Lisberger sets up a shot with actors Jeff Bridges and Bruce Boxleitner (c. 1982).

Jeff Bridges and Bruce Boxleitner film the live-action sequences for *Tron* at the Disney Studio in Burbank (c. 1981).

hand-tinting, or literally painting on the light. Much like Disney's traditional hand-drawn animation, this work was incredibly labor intensive. Looming production deadlines convinced the studio to ship the cel work to Taiwan, which worked out well but for one *tiny* glitch: when the cameramen opened the first batch of boxes, the cels were all stuck together—they'd been shipped before the paint was dry.

Tron's costume design was also deceptively simple. The cast wore black-and-white leotards with black Magic Marker "circuitry," hockey helmets, motocross pads, and Frisbees with black duct tape designs. Actor Bruce Boxleitner, who played the title character, recalled, "When they showed us the costumes, I said, 'You've got to be kidding. Where are the pants? Where are the pants?!'" The formfitting apparel also caused a stir around the Walt Disney Studios lot. "I know when we went to the commissary there was a thing that came down saying that would the actors please wear bathrobes, because [the costumes were] so skintight and we didn't have any pants on," Boxleitner said.

Old-fashioned shortcuts notwithstanding, *Tron* was the first movie in motion-picture history to use extensive computer-generated footage—more than twenty minutes in all. The studio brought in two leading computer imagery firms, Information International Inc. (Triple-I) and Mathematic Applications Group Inc. (MAGI) to assist with the digital scenes.

John Lasseter, the creator of 1995's *Toy Story*, the first computer-generated animated feature, was working on animated projects like *Mickey's Christmas Carol* when *Tron* was in production. "For me, this was some of the very first computer animation I had ever seen, and it was so exciting," he recalled. "The first scene that I remember them working on was the light-cycle sequence, and it absolutely blew me away. It was the perfect marriage of the technology and the subject matter. It was fantastic from that standpoint. So I think it really will always stand as one of the milestones of computer animation.

"Without *Tron*, there would be no *Toy Story*," added Lasseter, who would eventually become the creative head of both Disney and Pixar Animation Studios.

Surprisingly, the film was not nominated for an Oscar for its outstanding special effects work since, according to Lisberger, the Academy felt the production team cheated by using computers! "Things have certainly changed since then!" he remarked. *Tron* would also fail to drum up big box office numbers following its 1982 release, though it became something of a cultural touchstone, referenced decades later in shows like *Family Guy* and *South Park*. Disney would revisit the world with a long-awaited sequel, 2010's *Tron: Legacy*, which would earn a whopping $400 million worldwide and pave the way for an animated television series, *Tron: Uprising*, on the Disney XD network.

Elsewhere, Disney's overall creative funk began to infect even its animated features, where even popular offerings like *Robin Hood* (1973), *The Rescuers* (1977), and *The Fox and the Hound* (1981) lacked the storytelling magic fans had come to expect. It wasn't just the loss of Walt. Many of the old guard of animators and artists were now retired and the studio had no clear plan to nurture the new generation of artists it needed to replace them. Fortunately, an apprenticeship program was soon established through the California Institute of the Arts

(CalArts)—the art school largely funded through a generous endowment set up by Walt. The program allowed Walt's Nine Old Men and their contemporaries to groom the next generation of Disney animators. The transition was not without its struggles, however, as evidenced by the 1985 box office flop *The Black Cauldron*. The movie earned about $20 million and was tellingly eclipsed by a rerelease of the classic *One Hundred and One Dalmatians* the same year.

Not all the news of the era was grim, however. The early 1980s also brought significant milestones in Disney history, including the opening of two new theme parks, EPCOT Center and Tokyo Disneyland, and instantly popular attractions in other Disney parks, like *Space Mountain*, *Big Thunder Mountain Railroad*, and the Main Street Electrical Parade. The studio also introduced a second motion-picture label, Touchstone Pictures, and fulfilled a longtime dream of Walt's with the debut of its first TV network, The Disney Channel.

The new Touchstone banner provided an opportunity to produce mature, adult-centric films without tarnishing the family-friendly Disney brand. It got off to an auspicious start with the release of the smash hit *Splash* in 1984. Directed by Ron Howard and starring Tom Hanks and Daryl Hannah, *Splash* gave Disney

Disney CEO Ron Miller at a story conference for *The Black Cauldron* (in 1979).

The elaborate "South Seas Club" set constructed on Stage Two for *The Rocketeer* (c. 1989).

Behind the scenes on the 1987 Touchstone hit *Three Men and a Baby.*

its biggest opening weekend ever.

But such individual successes couldn't shake the perception—both in Hollywood and on Wall Street—that Walt Disney Productions was on shaky footing. In 1984, the studio faced two hostile takeover bids. Walt's nephew, Roy E., fearing his family's company would be carved up and sold to the highest bidder, quickly stepped in.

Roy E. urged the Board of Directors to install a new management team to lead the company; and they listened. On September 22, 1984, the board appointed Paramount Studios chief Michael D. Eisner as Disney's new chairman and chief executive officer, and highly respected Warner Bros. executive Frank G. Wells as the company's new president. Soon to be named The Walt Disney Company, the once-struggling studio began a three-decade long renaissance that catapulted it into the position of the world's foremost leader in high-quality family entertainment.

KEEP MOVING FORWARD

Disney Feature Animation staff poses for a division
photo in front of the Animation Building (1980s).

In 1984, Michael Eisner became Disney's chairman and CEO with Frank G. Wells serving as the company's president. Shortly after moving into Walt's old office suite in the Animation Building, Eisner, and Wells, made the most un-Walt type of decision: to move the Animation Department out.

Roy E. Disney, in a December 1984 memo to staff, said the division's transfer to the company's satellite location in nearby Glendale was intended to create "much needed office space...for our expanding live-action, motion-picture operations." It was a sobering, if not entirely surprising, move, for the former crown jewel of Disney's empire. However, the department had produced a string of costly, lackluster releases since Walt's death, including its current troubled production, *The Black Cauldron*, which would make back about half of its record-breaking budget. Roy, however, remained committed to the future of Disney Feature Animation and promised Eisner to personally take the group under his wing.

Ironically, the Studio would find almost immediate success with televised cartoons. Walt Disney Television Animation, established just two months after their arrival in November 1984, quickly produced a pair of hits: 1985's *Disney's Adventures of the Gummi Bears* and *Disney's Wuzzles*. Successful cartoon series like *DuckTales*, *Chip 'n' Dale Rescue Rangers*, *TaleSpin*, and *Darkwing Duck* would soon follow.

Disney's newly formed live-action Touchstone Television unit would also strike gold with its NBC sitcom *The Golden Girls*, which premiered in 1985. The show would run for seven seasons, win eleven Emmy Awards, and find new audiences in syndication, where it still airs today. Not a bad start for the new television production studio. The following year, *The Disney Sunday Movie* returned to ABC, now with Eisner serving as host, taping his weekly introductions on a studio soundstage.

On the feature film side, Touchstone Pictures released the box office hit *Down and Out in Beverly Hills* in 1986, starring Bette Midler and Richard Dreyfuss as Barbara and Dave Whiteman, which was shot primarily on the soundstages and back lot of Disney Studios. In fact, the crew constructed the Whiteman's posh

Beverly Hills home, complete with swimming pool, on Residential Street. Touchstone and Walt Disney Pictures would continue their successful run with live-action blockbusters like *The Color of Money*; *Who Framed Roger Rabbit*; *Good Morning, Vietnam*; *Three Men and a Baby*; *Beaches*; *Dead Poet's Society*; and *Honey, I Shrunk the Kids*.

Meanwhile, Disney's theme parks continued their remarkable growth: Disneyland opened the hugely popular *Splash Mountain* attraction in 1989, while Walt Disney World in Orlando added Typhoon Lagoon, its first water park; an all-new theme park experience, the Disney-MGM Studios (now Disney's Hollywood Studios); and its Pleasure Island nighttime entertainment district.

During this time, the company's market capitalization increased from $2 billion in 1984 to an incredible $16 billion in 1989. But all this success created a dilemma that Walt had known all-too-well: Disney had outgrown its fifty-one-acre studio lot. Eisner and Wells had anticipated this growth when they moved Animation and other departments to leased buildings around Burbank and Glendale.

One solution: the company began construction of its new Team Disney Building. Situated at the corner of Alameda and Buena Vista streets, where Walt's staffers once played baseball and golf in their downtime, the six-story, 334,100-square-foot corporate headquarters was designed by leading postmodernist architect Michael Graves.

Team Disney featured spacious, beautifully appointed suites, particularly on the sixth floor, where top executives would have offices; outdoor courtyards with sweeping, formal arcades; an expansive reflecting pool; four separate screening rooms; and The Rotunda, the appropriately named executive dining room located within the building's crowning architectural flourish.

The exterior's earth-tone color palate, which complemented the adjacent Animation Building, required ninety-five thousand square feet of reddish sandstone from India, twenty-two thousand square feet of Mexican quarry tile, and twenty thousand square feet of French limestone. Graves initially suggested a whimsical

Disney touch—the figures of Pluto or Donald Duck being sprayed with water in the reflecting pool—but that was vetoed by Eisner. However, the architect persisted, feeling the building looked too much like a bank, and finally settled on a new idea: seven dwarfs instead of the seven classic Ionic or Doric columns that would have supported the roof.

And so—from Happy to Grumpy—Snow White's beloved dwarfs were created by the Walt Disney Imagineering Sculpture Studio under the careful supervision of John Hench. Made of fiberglass and concrete, with an internal steel structure, these up to nineteen-foot-tall, thirty-thousand-pound "pillars" supported the new Team Disney Building, and served as an appropriate homage to the movie which had funded the construction of the Burbank studio precisely fifty years earlier. The smallest dwarf, Dopey, who stands at twelve feet tall, sat atop the fifth floor, literally holding up the rafters.

Dedicated in 1990, Disney's new $28.6 million headquarters served as a major architectural landmark. *New York Times* critic Paul Goldberg called it "visually seductive," and *Time* magazine reported, "Perhaps it might be called pop surrealism that uses classic design elements the way Walt Disney cartoons used the physiognomy of a rodent to create Mickey Mouse." On January 23, 2006, following Eisner's retirement from Disney, the building would be rededicated as The Michael D. Eisner Building to honor his twenty-one years of leadership.

Working on the Team Disney Building made Graves "more lighthearted, less pompous," the architect acknowledged. "The Disney projects are a lot of fun, and architecture needs fun if it isn't to get too portentous." His achievement would have a great impact within the company, sparking a new style known as "entertainment architecture."

"I think it makes you smile, which I think is good for our company," Eisner said in describing the structure's aesthetic. "If it makes you gag, then I think we've gone too far. But I think our buildings make you smile." The CEO would later recruit other leading architects, including Robert A. M. Stern, Frank Gehry, Robert Venturi, and Arata Isozaki, to design Disney hotels, offices, and other projects around the world.

Michael Graves's Team Disney Building, with original reflecting pool (1992).

On November 6, 1991, the studio announced the next phase of its expansion plan, a $600 million, 1.97 million-square-foot overhaul of the Burbank lot meant to "reestablish the 'college-type' creative atmosphere envisioned by Walt." The comprehensive project called for four to six new soundstages, production facilities, an employee center, a creative arts center, and a casting building. The additions would result in more than five thousand employees returning to the lot.

"We've outgrown our current facilities," Alan Epstein, vice president of the Disney Development Company, told the *Burbank Leader* newspaper, noting that the company's feature film output had risen from two movies in 1984 to seventeen by 1990. Television production had also increased dramatically, with eleven series in production in 1991. Disney's five soundstages simply weren't enough, particularly when competitors like nearby Warner Bros., Universal, and Paramount operated up to twenty soundstages.

On May, 6, 1991, The Walt Disney Company joined the prestigious Dow Jones Industrial Average, capping a series of creative successes that included the start of a second motion-picture label, Hollywood Pictures, the

year before. The new banner's first release, *Arachnophobia*, which was shot partly on Stage Two, became a critical and commercial hit, a strong start for the new division of the studio. Touchstone Television continued to produce popular sitcoms such as *Boy Meets World* and the hugely successful *Home Improvement*, which filmed for many years in front of a live audience on Stage Four.

Perhaps the best news to come out of this period was the surprising reemergence of Disney's animated features department. True to his word, Roy E. Disney had succeeded in revitalizing the struggling division, a fact made abundantly clear with 1989's instant classic, *The Little Mermaid*. A throwback to the studio's fairy-tale-based early works, the movie would usher in a second Golden Age for Walt Disney Feature Animation that continued with *Beauty and the Beast* in 1991 and *Aladdin* in 1992.

As a symbol of the team's return to prominence, the company announced plans for a new, state-of-the-art animation studio just before *Aladdin*'s release. The three-story, 243,000-square-foot building would be built adjacent to the studio lot, on the site Walt had originally planned for his "Mickey Mouse" kiddie park. The six hundred animation

Chairman of the Board Michael D. Eisner and President Frank G. Wells (c. 1984).

An aerial view of the Walt Disney Studios in 1998.

artists scattered throughout six warehouses in adjacent Glendale since 1986 could now return home. "I think if there ever was a group that deserved a new building in American business, this group of artists deserve their own building," Eisner said at the time. "The company has a right to say we're here. We don't have to be hidden in a warehouse anymore."

New York architect Robert A. M. Stern designed the studio, envisioning a free-flowing, loftlike environment suited to creative chaos and social interaction. "I don't want a showplace. I want a workplace," Eisner told Stern. The architect sought to reflect the influences of Kem Weber's art moderne style and touches of Los Angeles architecture like the Pan Pacific Auditorium. He also found inspiration in Disney's rich library of classic animated features, landing on the magical hat from the "Sorcerer's Apprentice" sequence of *Fantasia* as the building's signature icon. "The whole idea of making a movie has been sorcery to me. So I wanted this building to express magic," Stern explained.

An eighty-four-foot-tall version of Mickey's sorcerer hat, complete with a crescent moon and stars (that was surrounded by the word A N I M A T I O N in giant stainless steel letters), was designed to sit above the building's main entrance. Not simply an architectural flourish, the hat would house the ceremonial—and vertiginous—office of Disney vice chairman, Roy E. Disney.

Work began on the $54 million Animation Building in May 1993 before design details were even complete, and the building opened December of the following year. The interior featured generous spaces with wide, open hallways, gaping skylights, and floor-to-ceiling windows; a five-story atrium with terrazzo floors; a 139-seat theater; and a reception area anchored by a circular maple desk showcasing 5,736 silhouettes of Mickey's head carved into the surface.

The building's main entrance boasted brick pilasters reminiscent of classic movie theaters, and the fanciful exterior was emblazoned with

fourteen-foot-tall letters that again spelled out the word A N I M A T I O N—in large enough size to be seen from the nearby 134 Freeway. Orange and red corrugated metal soared above the building in a "Mohawk" or sail-like form, a uniquely iconic element that also served a practical purpose by concealing mechanical equipment on the roof. The art moderne style was also reflected in nautical touches like the porthole windows and open balconies resembling the decks of a 1930s ocean liner, particularly when lit at night.

"It brings back the liberating spirit of play that prevailed in the early years of postmodernism," noted *New York Times* architecture critic Herbert Duchamp. "The building itself is a cheerful collage, a jolly collision of spaces and symbols dedicated to the serious work of being silly. The building is a factory, an industrial plant for fun. In Mr. Stern's Disney Feature Animation Building, we're borne aloft on bright balloons of mirth."

Animation staff moved into their new building in late 1994 and set to work on new projects like *Pocahontas* and *The Hunchback of Notre Dame*. On May 7, 2010, the building was rededicated as the Roy E. Disney Animation Building, an honor bestowed upon the department's champion nearly five months after his death.

Despite the addition of yet another remarkable building and the wild success of the then new animated feature *The Lion King*, 1994 was a challenging year for Disney. President Frank Wells died in a tragic helicopter crash during a ski trip on April 3, and Studio Chairman Jeffrey Katzenberg abruptly left the company following a failed bid to replace him. Eisner also faced a serious health scare, leading to bypass surgery. Meanwhile, the company was forced to abandon plans for a U.S. history-based theme park in Virginia called Disney's America and dealt with the fallout of serious financial troubles with its new Euro Disney resort (now known as Disneyland Paris).

Robert A. M. Stern's fanciful 243,000-square-foot Feature Animation Studios Building (1994).

ABC Riverside Building.

Sharing the Magic of Roy O. and Minnie in Legends Plaza.

But the following year, four decades to the month after the opening of Disneyland, the American Broadcasting Company (ABC), which had been an investor in and one-third owner of Walt's then new theme park, was acquired by The Walt Disney Company. The $19 billion merger of Disney and Capital Cities/ABC, which was announced on July 31, 1995, would forever change the landscape of the company that Walt had built.

Disney's growing portfolio of entertainment offerings would now include the ABC Television Network (and under that a national broadcaster and regional television stations—and the same with radio stations), publishing interests, and stakes in several major cable networks, including a majority position in the sports behemoth ESPN. The acquisition also brought Robert A. Iger, then chairman of ABC, to Disney; ten years later he would become chief executive officer of The Walt Disney Company.

Given the incredible growth and activity seen throughout the Disney organization, it was clear that the studio's 1991 master plan, which had

Roy E. Disney inside his "Sorcerer's Hat" office in the Feature Animation Studios Building (1994).

Disney Legends Plaza (2017).

Frank G. Wells Building (2015).

not yet been fully realized, would call for further
expansion. The next phase of construction came
in 1997, when two new soundstages, Stages
Six and Seven, were completed. At fifteen
thousand square feet each, these state-of-the-art
production facilities—which boasted the latest
acoustics, technical, and operational advances—
were the first new stages to be added at the
Disney Studio in thirty-five years. A six-story
production support building was also included as
part of the project requirements; the new facility
offered ample rehearsal space, production offices,
dressing rooms, and edit bays. The new stages
were primarily used to produce television series
such as the hit ABC drama *Brothers & Sisters*.
Also completed that year was a new business
street facade that was a small but versatile area,
which could easily be decorated to resemble any
time period or part of the country. The sets were
ideal for outdoor shots required predominantly
for television productions.

The following year, two major additions to
the studio lot were dedicated on October 16,
1998, the date of the company's seventy-fifth
anniversary. First was Legends Plaza, the new
location that would honor those recognized with
the prestigious Disney Legends Award. The
plaza was built on the site of the reflecting pool
situated in front of the Team Disney Building.

The new space was immediately embraced
by both Disney employees and admirers, as
the plaza became a stirring reminder of the
imagination and creative talents of the men and
women who had made Disney magic during

the company's first three quarters of a century.
The centerpiece of the plaza was the fourteen-
foot enlargement of the actual Disney Legends
Award. Sculpted by former Imagineer Andrea
Favilli, and made in Pietrasanta, Italy, the
sculpture weighs 1,652 pounds; those who take
the time to look closely at it may discover some
hidden treasures that cannot be found on the
smaller-scale statue, such as Gus from *Cinderella*.
The plaza now also featured the bronze *Partners*
statue, with Walt and Mickey; the *Sharing the
Magic* statue, with Roy O. Disney and Minnie
Mouse sitting on a bench; and newly designed
personalized plaques adorning the pillars
surrounding the plaza, which were created
for each Disney Legend (and many of which
displayed their handprints and signature).

Also dedicated that day was the new Frank
G. Wells Building, situated in the northwest
corner of the studio adjacent to Legends Plaza
and occupying the same footprint as some of
the former back lot areas. As president and chief
operating officer of The Walt Disney Company
from 1984 until his untimely passing in 1994,
Wells was instrumental in helping to transform
Disney into the phenomenally successful
entertainment conglomerate that it had become,
and honoring his memory in this way seemed
an appropriate homage. During the ceremony,
Eisner said of his friend and business partner,
"Those who knew Frank well could describe
him as elegant, intelligent, friendly, thoughtful,
and practical. These are the attributes that are
embodied in this building we dedicate today." At
the front entrance of the building is a dedication

147

continued on page 151

PIRATES OF THE CARIBBEAN

Johnny Depp and Orlando Bloom float through the watery *Pirates of the Caribbean* cave set on Stage Two (2002).

CEO Bob Iger on the set of *Pirates of the Caribbean: Dead Man's Chest.*

In 2001, former Disney Studio chairman Dick Cook's office received a call from Johnny Depp's agent requesting a meeting. "I've got two little kiddies, and I realize that all they do is watch Disney movies," the actor told him when they talked. I would like to do something my kids would like to see. And most of what I've done in my career isn't really appropriate for them."

Depp proceeded to list his children's favorite Disney movies— *Cinderella* and *Bambi* to *Robin Hood* and *Beauty and the Beast*—so Cook assumed he wanted to voice an animated character. But the actor's interest lay in live action, even if Disney's upcoming slate of films didn't offer a particularly good fit. The studio chairman offered one last project: "Well, we don't have a script yet—it's simply an idea—but we have a little two-page treatment for a story based on the *Pirates of the Caribbean* ride at Disneyland," he said. "It's a three-hander . . . two guys and a girl. One of them is a rogue pirate."

Depp lifted up his hand and asked, "With a sword? I'll do it." And just like that, the *Pirates of the Caribbean* franchise had its Captain Jack Sparrow. Renowned producer Jerry Bruckheimer would soon sign on, as would Director Gore Verbinski, but "Johnny was first to know about our *Pirates* movie and the first to say he wanted to be in it," Cook noted. "He made *Pirates of the Caribbean* extraordinary. He's an iconic character now."

Before production began, a full-size version of Sparrow's pirate vessel, *The Black Pearl,* was built on Stage One for ship interiors and close-up shots, while Stage Two became the cavernous Treasure Cave. "The cave set is one of the largest sets ever built on a stage in Hollywood, and it's a centerpiece in the movie because that's where the cursed treasure is hidden," said Executive Producer Bruce Hendricks. More than a hundred craftsmen spent about five months building the set using wood frame,

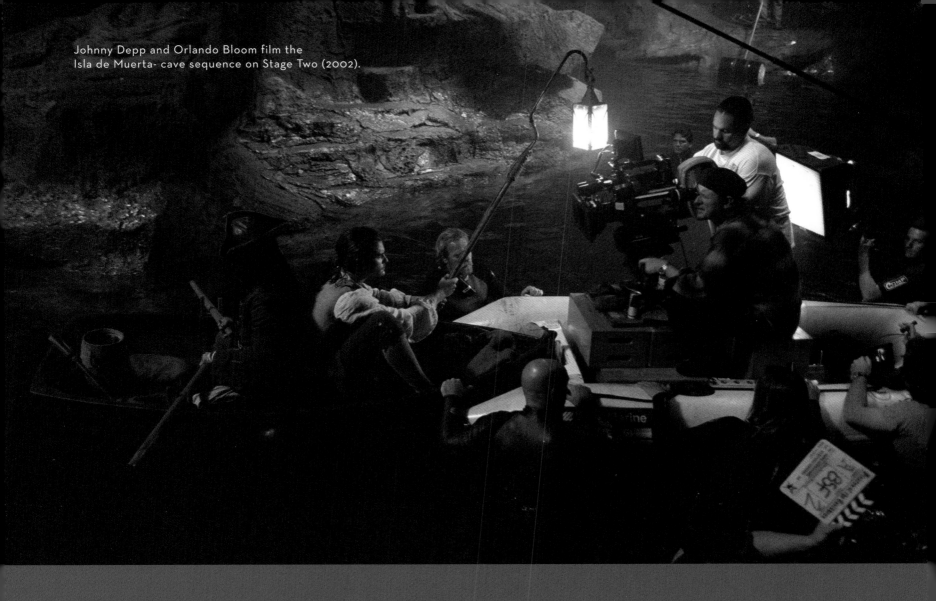

Johnny Depp and Orlando Bloom film the Isla de Muerta- cave sequence on Stage Two (2002).

plaster, and Styrofoam.

Set decorator Larry Dias called the Treasure Cave "one of the bigger challenges of the entire film. . . . I can't even think of how many cubic feet of rock that we actually painted to look like gold nuggets, as well as hundreds of yards of pearls and a mass of odd objects, things that would just be looted by the pirates."

Verbinski's desire for authenticity and detail rivaled that of Walt's in his prime, whether it meant procuring an actual mid-eighteenth-century pistol with silver inlay for Captain Jack or fabricating the nine hundred-plus costumes needed for the cast. "I didn't want these pirates to be hooks-for-hands, eye patches, and trick-or-treat belts and striped shirts and all that," he explained. "Basically, they were rotting human beings. There was very little time to live, and you had scurvy and the ships leaked, and there were rats

everywhere, and there's kind of [a] really fun, disgusting quality and texture to that."

To achieve the desired effect, costume designer Penny Rose rented a cement mixer, put the costumes in it, and let it run, creating just the tattered, worn, and filthy pirate apparel the director wanted.

Premiering on July 9, 2003, *Pirates of the Caribbean: The Curse of the Black Pearl* earned $650 million in global box office receipts and spawned five highly profitable sequels. Many elements of the second and third installments were shot on the Disney lot, including those from Tia Dalma's mysterious bayou environs, Davy Jones's forbidding *Flying Dutchman* ghost ship from *Dead Man's Chest* and the treacherous pirate lair Shipwreck Island for *At World's End*. The fourth and fifth installments, *On Stranger Tides* and *Dead Men Tell No Tales* were shot mostly on location in exotic ports of call far from Burbank.

And speaking of exotic locations through the years, Jack Sparrow and other characters from the films have made their way into the iconic theme park attraction, with Audio-Animatronics versions of Jack popping up at Disneyland, Walt Disney World, Disneyland Paris, and Tokyo Disneyland. In 2016, the *Pirates of the Caribbean* story came full circle when a brand-new version of the original beloved Disneyland attraction debuted at Shanghai Disneyland as *Pirates of the Caribbean: Battle for the Sunken Treasure*. "*Pirates of the Caribbean* is one of the most iconic attractions in our parks, and we really couldn't imagine Shanghai Disneyland without Pirates," said Bob Iger. "We wanted to create a one-of-a-kind experience that would appeal to our Chinese guests while remaining true to its Disney heritage."

THE WALT DISNEY ARCHIVES

Founder of the Walt Disney Archives, David R. Smith (2010).

The Walt Disney Archives, which was established by Dave Smith in 1970, is responsible for preserving and sharing Disney's vast and storied history and legacy. The department maintains an exhaustive collection of documentation and artifacts from Walt Disney and other prominent Disney executives; an impressive collection of artwork, props, costumes, and set pieces from Disney's most prominent films, television programs, and theme parks; an extensive assortment of vintage and contemporary Disney collectibles, merchandise, and books; millions of images in its Photo Library, including 8,500 photos of Walt; and much more. A small selection of the Archives' treasures is on a rotating display in the Frank G. Wells Building's lobby and in the Archives' main research room and offices, all of which remain popular destinations for guests and dignitaries visiting the Walt Disney Studios.

The Walt Disney Archives, located on the first floor of the Frank G. Wells Building (2015).

plaque that illustrates the great esteem of Frank's Disney coworkers. It features a quote from *Lincoln, Man of the People* by Edwin Markham: "Here was a man to hold against the world, a man to match the mountains and the sea as when a lordly cedar green with boughs goes down with a great shout upon the hills, and leaves a lonesome place against the sky." At the very bottom of the plaque is a phrase that Frank himself used as a life motto: "Humility is the Final Achievement."

Designed by world-renowned architect Robert Venturi, the five-story, 270,000-square-foot Frank G. Wells Building featured oversized film-reel designs on the front facade, interior atrium walls painted to resemble shafts of light from movie premiere klieg lights, and a lobby decorated in shades of black and white to reflect a black-and-white film motif. After passing through the lobby, Venturi would introduce guests to the world of "color," which would adorn the building's office spaces.

The Wells building included a 112-seat screening room, the studio's main mail and warehouse facility, a quad multipurpose room, office space, and three levels of subterranean parking. The building's original occupants included the Touchstone Pictures Casting Department, Walt Disney Television Animation, various television and feature film production units, Disney New Technology, the Disney University, Human Resources, and the Walt Disney Archives.

During 1998, the company also announced that ABC's headquarters would be moved from New York City to Burbank, bringing the group's management and operations onto the same studio lot as its new parent company. To house the three hundred to four hundred ABC employees moving from the East Coast, a new ten-story, 390,000-square-foot building would be required. The "modern classic" structure would be located across Riverside Drive from the main studio lot and next door to the Feature Animation Building.

Designed by Italian architect Aldo Rossi and American architect Morris Adjmi, the new ABC Riverside Building, as it would be called, incorporated a color palate and design consistent with the art deco theme of the studio's classic

The new Walt Disney Studios Motion Pictures Film Archive Building (2015).

Kem Weber designed/influenced buildings. The building's unique design would, however, give the appearance of a streetscape of three buildings rather than one. The tower that rises from the building's west side was capped with a decorative art deco–inspired lantern affixed with the iconic ABC logo.

The new ABC headquarters opened fall 2000 and contained office space, a full commissary, large conference rooms, screening rooms, five levels of underground parking, and an artfully illuminated pedestrian bridge connecting the building to the studio's main campus across Riverside Drive.

In the new millennium, Disney has continued on its path of rapid growth. Under the leadership of Bob Iger, the company has significantly expanded its legendary creativity and innovation, particularly with the strategic acquisitions of Pixar Animation Studios, home to Woody, Buzz Lightyear, Nemo, Lightning McQueen, and the Incredibles; Marvel Entertainment, which boasts such Super Heroes as Iron Man, Black Panther, Thor, Captain America, and the Hulk; and Lucasfilm, with Darth Vader, Luke Skywalker, and the entire *Star Wars* universe of characters. Released in December 2015, *Star Wars: The Force Awakens* would go on to become the number one box office hit in U.S. history. Iger's talent for making strategic acquisitions and expanding key franchises helped increase Disney's market capitalization from $48.8 billion when he became CEO in October of 2005 to $167 billion at the

The dedication of the newly restored Walt Disney Office Suite by CEO Bob Iger and three of Walt's granddaughters on Dec. 7, 2015. Left to right: Michelle Lund, Jennifer Goff, Joanna Miller, and Bob Iger.

end of fiscal 2018. In 2017, Disney agreed to the biggest acquisition in its history with the purchase of 21st Century Fox, including such acclaimed businesses as Twentieth Century Fox, Fox Searchlight Pictures, the FX Network, and National Geographic Partners.

Under Iger, Disney Animation has created a string of blockbuster hits, including *Tangled*, *Wreck-It Ralph*, *Zootopia*, and the incomparable *Frozen*— the number one animated film of all time. Disney live-action films have also flourished, building upon Walt's legacy with the swashbuckling *Pirates of the Caribbean* films, *Tim Burton's Alice in Wonderland*, *Maleficent*, *Cinderella*, *The Jungle Book*, and *Beauty and the Beast*. The studio lot even had its own "cameo" in the film *Saving Mr. Banks*, in which Tom Hanks portrays Walt Disney during the years that he struggled with author P. L. Travers over the creation of a film based on her popular books about a nanny named Mary Poppins. Using actual exterior locations on the studio lot, and faithful re-creations of Walt Disney's offices, the film gives audiences a fascinating glimpse into what it was like to work on the Burbank lot in the 1960s.

The Marvel Cinematic Universe has produced enormous hits, including the *Iron Man* trilogy, the *Thor* and *Captain America* films, *Dr. Strange*, *Guardians of the Galaxy Volumes 1 and 2*, and, of course, *Marvel's The Avengers*, *Avengers: Age of Ultron*, and *Avengers: Infinity War*.

ABC Studios (formerly Touchstone Television) has created a host of popular series for the ABC Television Network, including *Grey's Anatomy*, *Once Upon a Time*, *Desperate Housewives*, and *Lost*, as well as several hits produced on the studio lot, including *Alias*, *Brothers & Sisters*, *black-ish*, and *grown-ish*.

Since the turn of the twenty-first century, Disney has opened brand-new theme parks around the world, including the never-before-seen world of wonder that is Shanghai Disneyland, Hong Kong Disneyland, Tokyo DisneySea, and Disney California Adventure. New lands and spectacular attractions have been created at all of its parks, delighting guests with new adventures and thrills. And the popular Disney Cruise Line fleet has grown to include four luxury liners, with three more on the way.

Since its beginnings, the story of The Walt Disney Company has been one of imagination, magic, growth, and success. And, as in its earliest years, the studio's physical locations have had to stretch to accommodate the limitless creativity of the men and women who work here.

As Disney has expanded beyond Walt's collaborative, campus-like environment, Iger recognized the need to create locations for Disney employees that are dynamic, inspirational, and conducive to the creative process. The realization of this vision had its most profound manifestation in 2006 when the majority of Disney employees occupying leased space in the Burbank and Glendale, California, area was consolidated into what became known as the Grand Central Creative Campus. This location was once occupied by the Grand Central Airport, the first airport in Los Angeles and a key place in the history of United States aviation. After the airport closed in 1959, it was redeveloped as an industrial park, consisting largely of low-lying tilt-up buildings—and it was there that WED Enterprises (now Walt Disney Imagineering) moved in 1961 and has remained ever since.

The Grand Central Creative Campus is rapidly becoming a "second studio lot," as many employees call it, and it has the campus-like atmosphere that would no doubt have pleased Walt. The new area features buildings that were constructed with modern architectural precepts, including raised floor ventilation systems and highly efficient air-conditioning and lighting,

making them particularly flexible, efficient, and sustainable. The buildings also have their own unique Disney identity, with exteriors featuring art glass imagery surrounded by open patios and shady palm tree–lined avenues. Both indoors and out, there are comfortable corners that are conducive to idea sharing. Whimsical touches also abound, including a kinetic Mickey Mouse-themed fountain and various life-sized Disney character figures, which dot the campus. This new vibrant and energetic creative center is headquarters to Walt Disney Imagineering, Disney's consumer products business, Walt Disney Television Animation, the KABC television station (serving the whole Los Angeles area), the Walt Disney Archives Photo Library, Disney Corporate Creative Resources, and D23: The Official Disney Fan Club, among others.

In April 2013, Glendale's Historic Preservation Commission voted unanimously to approve The Walt Disney Company's plan to restore the most historic building in the area, the Grand Central Air Terminal. The terminal building and control tower, which opened in 1929, were designed by architect Henry L. Gogerty, who combined Spanish colonial revival with art deco and streamline moderne influences. Work on the building, which included a faithful restoration of the beautiful exterior and significant interior spaces, was completed in late 2015. The building is now a multipurpose facility, with offices, event space, and a visitors' center that celebrates the rich history of the building and the important role it played in aviation history.

The restored Grand Central Air Terminal's exterior and interior (2015).

Grand Central Creative Campus in Glendale.

While The Walt Disney Company's diversified, far-reaching global operations have grown too large to be housed entirely at its fifty-one-acre Burbank headquarters, this historic and legendary site has and will always remain the epicenter of Disney imagination and its creative heart. Perhaps it is the ever-present buzz of production, the iconic water tower (with its image of Mickey Mouse), the fanciful Seven Dwarfs overlooking Legends Plaza, or the spirit of Walt that can often be felt—particularly when visiting his restored office suite in the northeast corner of the old Animation Building. Even today while walking on the lot, one can't help but glance up at Walt's office on the third floor, as if hoping to catch a glimpse of the company's founder overseeing his bustling studio operations.

Whether it's the revolutionary achievements in entertainment, regular star sightings, the friendly squirrels, or just the excitement of Disney magic, there is something special about the Walt Disney Studios. But it's more than a place where motion-picture history was made or theme park elements were constructed. It's home to the timeless stories, beloved characters, unforgettable songs, and enchanting memories that remain in our hearts and minds forever. These warm feelings and experiences are passed down like cherished family heirlooms to our children and our grandchildren, generation after generation. And for those fortunate enough to stroll across the serene, parklike setting of the studio, one can perhaps sense the culmination of that magic, as much as one can envision the studio's namesake traversing the lot he once reigned over as its master storyteller.

As the Walt Disney Studios approaches the eightieth anniversary of its arrival in Burbank, it's with pause that we recognize that more years have passed without Walt on the lot than with him here at the creative hub he established—and nourished. But in those first twenty-six years he spent presiding over his Burbank studio, Walt laid the firm foundation that continues to inspire and guide those afforded the honor and deep responsibility of carrying on the founder's vision, pioneering spirit, and rich legacy into new centuries and new frontiers.

As Walt said, "There's really no secret to our approach. We keep moving forward—opening new doors and doing new things—because we're curious. And curiosity keeps leading us down new paths."

The Walt Disney Studios back lot (2015).

AFTERWORD

In little more than a decade after Walt Disney created Mickey Mouse, his good fortunes found him moving into a brand-new, $2 million dream factory, consisting of twenty-one buildings on a fifty-one-acre tract of land in a sleepy corner of California's San Fernando Valley. It wasn't sleepy for long.

From its beginnings in 1940, the Disney Studio in Burbank quickly came to symbolize its founder's dedication to realizing dreams, no matter how impossible or insurmountable they seemed. More than an entertainment pioneer, studio chief, or movie mogul, Walt Disney was a storyteller who created lasting memories of beauty, wonder, and significance for people everywhere. And for his dedicated artists and innovators, he constructed this idyllic haven, built for the purpose of creating unforgettable enchantments that touch the heart, tickle the funny bone, inspire a song, or ignite the imagination.

Seventy-five years after opening its gates, the Burbank studio continues to represent the optimism, hope, humor, goodwill, and heart that its founding visionary spent his entire life pursuing. And whether you've worked at the studio, had the opportunity to be a visitor, or are simply captivated by the knowledge of its legendary existence, the Walt Disney Studios has most certainly given all of us a *lot* to remember.

The Walt Disney Studios (2015).

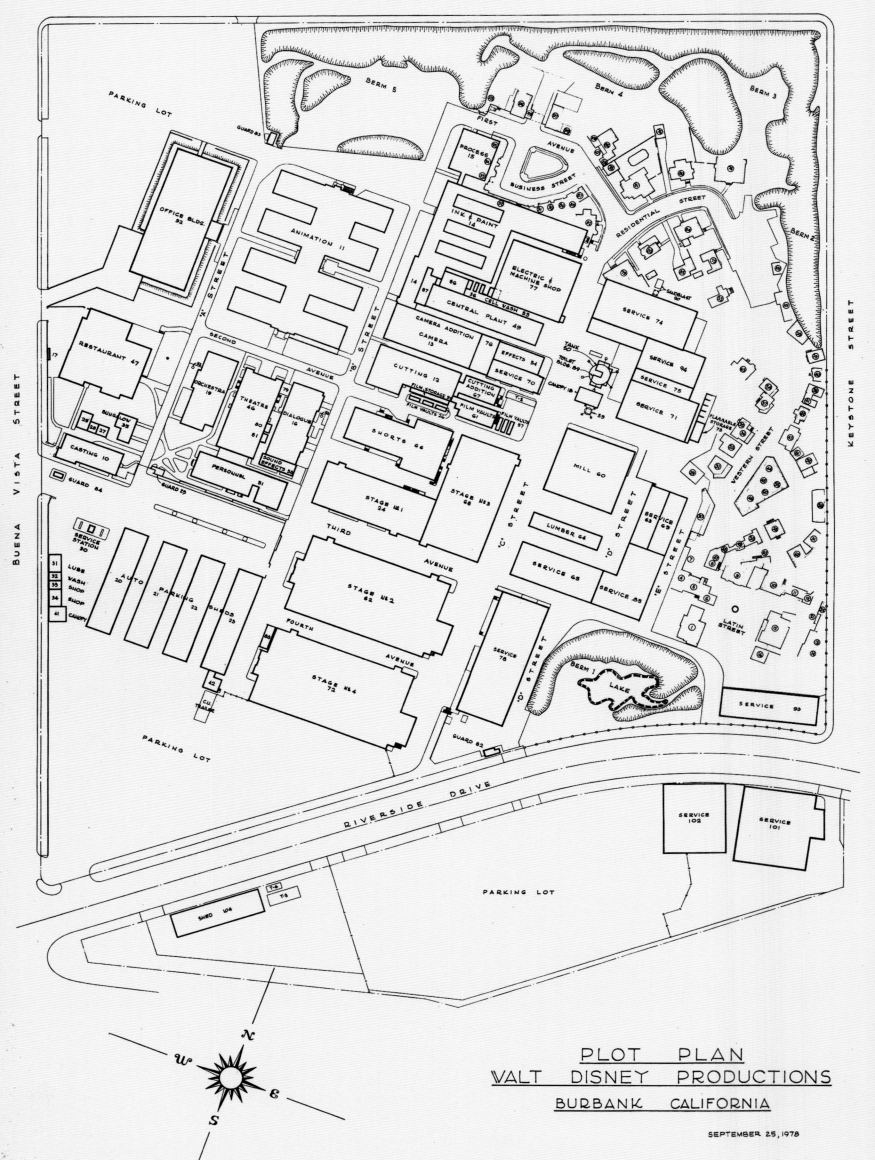

ALAMEDA AVENUE

PLOT PLAN
VALT DISNEY PRODUCTIONS
BURBANK CALIFORNIA

SEPTEMBER 25, 1978

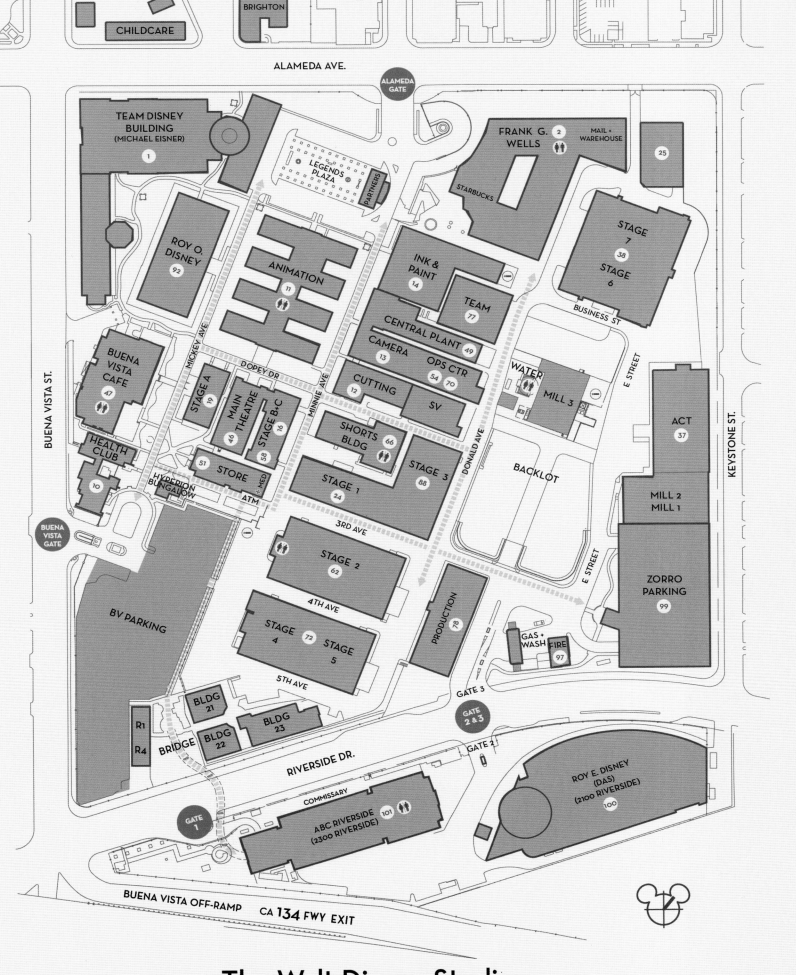

The Walt Disney Studio
500 South Buena Vista Street, Burbank

MAP & DIRECTIONS

* Guests please use RIVERSIDE GATE 3
Park in Zorro parking structure

Directions from 134 fwy (North bound)
Take Buena Vista Street exit from 134 fwy

Directions from 134 fwy (South bound)
Take Bob Hope Drive exit from 134 fwy
Turn right onto Bob Hope Dr.
Take first left onto Riverside Dr.

ACKNOWLEDGMENTS

Throughout the history of Disney—and most endeavors in life—few achievements or accomplishments are arrived at alone. As such, it is the support and contributions of many thoughtful and insightful people who helped make this book possible.

A special thanks to the thousands of men, women, and children who have contributed so profoundly to the Disney legacy over the last century and, more specifically, to the Disney Studios over the past seventy-five years. We would also like to recognize the entire staff of the Walt Disney Archives and Photo Library for their assistance, as well as our friends Laura Hopper, Jessica Ward, Jennifer Eastwood, Winnie Ho, and Margie Peng at Disney Publishing, who helped make this book a reality. Thanks also to Kevin Luperchio for his insight and contribution.

Above all, we thank our families and loved ones: Kenneth and Harriett Clark, Alfonso Zavala, Ilean Ochoa, Michele Ochoa, David Clark, Amy Hossfeld, Zenia Mucha, Hope Hartman, and, of course, Maggie, Andy, and Jackson.

Lastly, we extend our deepest thanks and appreciation to our friend, adviser, and editor-extraordinaire Wendy Lefkon. Her vast knowledge of Disney, her compassion in life, and her dedication to her colleagues and cohorts are the things we aspire to and admire.